NORTHSTAR 1

LISTENING AND SPEAKING

SECOND EDITION

AUTHORS
Polly Merdinger
Laurie Barton

SERIES EDITORS
Frank Boyd
Carol Numrich

PEARSON
Longman

Dedication

This book is dedicated to my husband Ricky, and our daughters Julia and Nina, who cannot remember a time in their lives when I was not writing *NorthStar*.

Polly Merdinger

I dedicate this book to my husband, Craig Binns, who took care of our children so that I could write.

Laurie Barton

NorthStar: Listening and Speaking Level 1, Second Edition

Copyright © 2009, 2003 by Pearson Education, Inc.
All rights reserved.

Pearson Education, 10 Bank Street, White Plains, NY 10606

Contributor credits: For *NorthStar: Listening and Speaking Level 1, Second Edition*, Natasha Haugnes authored material for Unit 10. Linda Lane, American Language Program at Columbia University, authored and edited all PRONUNCIATION material.

Staff credits: The people who made up the *NorthStar: Listening and Speaking Level 1, Second Edition* team, representing editorial, production, design, and manufacturing, are Camelot Editorial Services LLC, Aerin Csigay, Dave Dickey, Ann France, Dana Klinek, Melissa Leyva, Sherry Preiss, Robert Ruvo, Debbie Sistino, and Paula Van Ells.

Cover art: Silvia Rojas/Getty Images
Text composition: Elect____ ____hics, Inc.
Text font: 12.5/14 Mini____
Credits: See page 239.

Library of Congress Cataloging-in-Publication Data

Merdinger, Polly.
    NorthStar. Level 1 : listening and speaking / Polly Merdinger and
Laurie Barton. — 2nd ed.
        p. cm.
    Rev. ed. of: Northstar : focus on listening and speaking, introductory,
/ Polly Merdinger, Laurie Barton, 2003.
    Includes bibliographical references.
    ISBN-13: 978-0-13-613335-3 (student text bk : alk. paper)
    ISBN-10: 0-13-613335-5 (student text bk : alk. paper)
    ISBN-13: 978-0-13-613338-4 (student text w/MyNorthStarLab)
    ISBN-13: 978-0-13-613337-7 (audio cd)
    [etc.]
    1. English language—Textbooks for foreign speakers. 2. English
language—Spoken English—Problems, exercises, etc. 3.
Listening—Problems, exercises, etc. I. Barton, Laurie. II. Title. III.
Title: Level 1, listening and speaking.
    PE1128.M444 2008
    428.2'4—dc22

                                                    2008024488

ISBN 10: 0-13-613335-5
ISBN 13: 978-0-13-613335-3

Printed in the United States of America
7 8 9 10—V011—13 12 11

CONTENTS

WELCOME TO NORTHSTAR

SECOND EDITION

NorthStar, now in its new edition, motivates students to succeed in their **academic** as well as **personal** language goals.

For each of the five levels, the two strands—*Reading and Writing* and *Listening and Speaking*—provide a fully integrated approach for students and teachers.

WHAT IS SPECIAL ABOUT THE NEW EDITION?

NEW THEMES

New themes and **updated content**—presented in a **variety of genres**, including literature and lectures, and in **authentic reading and listening selections**—challenge students intellectually.

ACADEMIC SKILLS

More purposeful **integration of critical thinking** and an enhanced focus on **academic skills** such as inferencing, synthesizing, note taking, and test taking help students develop strategies for **success** in the **classroom** and on **standardized tests**. A **culminating productive task** galvanizes content, language, and **critical thinking skills**.

➤ In the *Listening and Speaking* strand, a **structured approach** gives students opportunities for **more extended and creative oral practice**, for example, presentations, simulations, debates, case studies, and public service announcements.

➤ In the *Reading and Writing* strand, a new, **fully integrated writing section** leads students through the **writing process** with engaging writing assignments focusing on various rhetorical modes.

NEW DESIGN

Full **color pages** with more **photos, illustrations, and graphic organizers** foster student engagement and make the content and activities come alive.

MyNorthStarLab

MyNorthStarLab, an easy-to-use **online learning and assessment program**, offers:

➤ Unlimited access to reading and listening selections and DVD segments.

➤ Focused test preparation to help students succeed on international exams such as TOEFL® and IELTS®. Pre- and post-unit assessments improve results by providing individualized instruction, instant feedback, and personalized study plans.

➤ Original activities that support and extend the *NorthStar* program. These include pronunciation practice using voice recording tools, and activities to build note taking skills and academic vocabulary.

➤ Tools that save time. These include a flexible gradebook and authoring features that give teachers control of content and help them track student progress.

THE NORTHSTAR APPROACH

The *NorthStar* series is based on **current research in language acquisition** and on the **experiences of teachers and curriculum designers**. Five principles guide the *NorthStar* approach.

PRINCIPLES

1 **The more profoundly students are stimulated intellectually and emotionally, the more language they will use and retain.**

The thematic organization of *NorthStar* promotes intellectual and emotional stimulation. The 50 sophisticated themes in *NorthStar* present intriguing topics such as recycled fashion, restorative justice, personal carbon footprints, and microfinance. The authentic content engages students, links them to language use outside of the classroom, and encourages personal expression and critical thinking.

2 **Students can learn both the form and content of the language.**

Grammar, vocabulary, and culture are inextricably woven into the units, providing students with systematic and multiple exposures to language forms in a variety of contexts. As the theme is developed, students can express complex thoughts using a higher level of language.

3 **Successful students are active learners.**

Tasks are designed to be creative, active, and varied. Topics are interesting and up-to-date. Together these tasks and topics (1) allow teachers to bring the outside world into the classroom and (2) motivate students to apply their classroom learning in the outside world.

4 **Students need feedback.**

This feedback comes naturally when students work together practicing language and participating in open-ended opinion and inference tasks. Whole class activities invite teachers' feedback on the spot or via audio/video recordings or notes. The innovative new MyNorthStarLab gives students immediate feedback as they complete computer-graded language activities online; it also gives students the opportunity to submit writing or speaking assignments electronically to their instructor for feedback later.

5 **The quality of relationships in the language classroom is important because students are asked to express themselves on issues and ideas.**

The information and activities in *NorthStar* promote genuine interaction, acceptance of differences, and authentic communication. By building skills and exploring ideas, the exercises help students participate in discussions and write essays of an increasingly complex and sophisticated nature.

THE NORTHSTAR UNIT

① FOCUS ON THE TOPIC

This section introduces students to the unifying theme
of the listening selections.

> **PREDICT** and **SHARE INFORMATION** foster interest in the unit topic and help
> students develop a personal connection to it.
>
> **BACKGROUND** AND **VOCABULARY** activities provide students with tools for
> understanding the first listening selection. Later in the unit, students review
> this vocabulary and learn related idioms, collocations, and word forms. This
> helps them explore content and expand their written and spoken language.

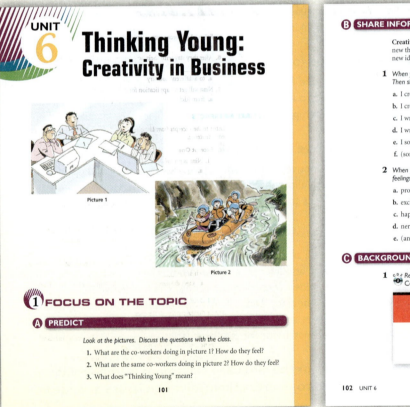

UNIT
6

Thinking Young:
Creativity in Business

Picture 1

Picture 2

① FOCUS ON THE TOPIC

A PREDICT

Look at the pictures. Discuss the questions with the class.

1. What are the co-workers doing in picture 1? How do they feel?
2. What are the same co-workers doing in picture 2? How do they feel?
3. What does "Thinking Young" mean?

101

B SHARE INFORMATION

Creative people have new and unusual ideas. Sometimes they create or make new things. Children are usually creative when they play. They have many new ideas.

1. *When you were a child, what creative thing(s) did you do? Circle your answers. Then share your answers with three classmates. Ask, "What did you do?"*

   a. I created a new game or toy.

   b. I created a piece of art (painting, sculpture).

   c. I wrote a song or played a musical instrument.

   d. I wrote a story or poem.

   e. I solved a problem in an unusual way.

   f. (something else?) _____

2. *When you were creative, how did you feel? Circle all the words that describe your feelings. Use your dictionary for help.*

   a. proud

   b. excited

   c. happy

   d. nervous

   e. (another feeling?) _____

C BACKGROUND AND VOCABULARY

1.  *Read and listen to the information from the business magazine Fast Company.*

Can Your Employees Learn to Be More Creative?
Many Business Owners Say "YES!"

Big companies, like American Express®, Microsoft®, FedEx Kinko's®, and Disney®, want their **employees** to be creative—to think in new and interesting ways. These companies pay billions of dollars for **creativity** classes for their employees.

102   UNIT 6

② FOCUS ON LISTENING

This section focuses on understanding two contrasting listening selections.

> **LISTENING ONE** is a radio report, interview, lecture, or other genre that addresses the unit topic. In levels 1 to 3, listenings are based on authentic materials. In levels 4 and 5, all the listenings are authentic.
>
> **LISTEN FOR MAIN IDEAS** and **LISTEN FOR DETAILS** are comprehension activities that lead students to an understanding and appreciation of the first selection.
>
> The **MAKE INFERENCES** activity prompts students to "listen between the lines," move beyond the literal meaning, exercise critical thinking skills, and understand the listening on a more academic level. Students follow up with pair or group work to discuss topics in the **EXPRESS OPINIONS** section.

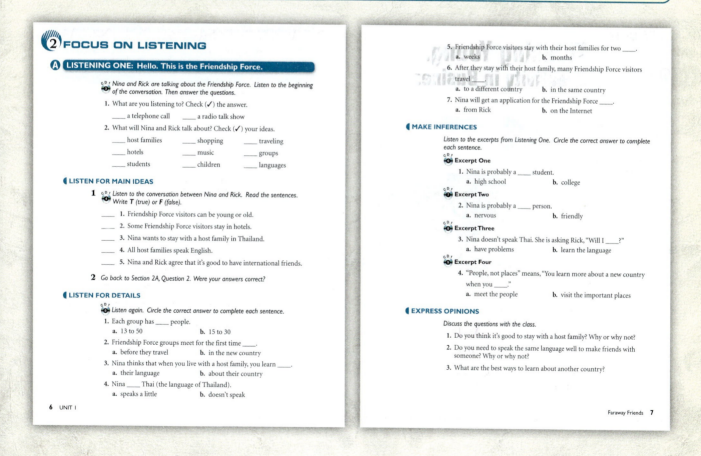

LISTENING TWO offers another perspective on the topic and is usually another genre. Again, in levels 1 to 3, the listenings are based on authentic materials and in levels 4 and 5, they are authentic. This second listening is followed by an activity that challenges students to question ideas they formed about the first listening, and to use appropriate language skills to analyze and explain their ideas.

INTEGRATE LISTENINGS ONE AND TWO presents culminating activities. Students are challenged to take what they have learned, organize the information, and synthesize it in a meaningful way. Students practice skills that are essential for success in authentic academic settings and on standardized tests.

---

4. I don't like to spend money on clothing. I don't think it's necessary to spend a lot of money on pants or a dress.

_____ Agree

_____ Disagree

5. I want to be a fashion designer. I think making new clothes is very exciting.

_____ Agree

_____ Disagree

B **LISTENING TWO: The Quilts of Gee's Bend**

Gee's Bend is the name of a small town in Alabama. The women of Gee's Bend are famous for their quilts. They use old materials to make beautiful quilts.

C **INTEGRATE LISTENINGS ONE AND TWO**

◀ **STEP 1: Organize**

Answer the questions in the chart. Use information from Listenings One and Two.

USING RECYCLED MATERIALS		
	Deborah Lindquist	**Gee's Bend Women**
1. What do they do?	Makes trendy clothes with unusual materials; makes eco-fashion	
2. Why do they use recycled materials?		
3. Where do they live?		

◀ **STEP 2: Synthesize**

Imagine that Deborah Lindquist from Listening One and the Gee's Bend woman from Listening Two are speaking to a news reporter.

1 Role-play. Work in groups of three. Complete the conversation with information from Step 1: Organize.

REPORTER: What do you make?
LINDQUIST: I make . . .
GEE'S BEND WOMAN: Well, I don't make . . .
REPORTER: Why do you use recycled materials?
GEE'S BEND WOMAN: I use them because . . .
LINDQUIST: I use recycled materials . . .

2 Practice responding to the questions. Then share one question and the answer with the class.

---

③ FOCUS ON SPEAKING

This section emphasizes development of productive skills for speaking. It includes sections on vocabulary, grammar, pronunciation, functional language, and an extended speaking task.

The **VOCABULARY** section leads students from reviewing the unit vocabulary, to practicing and expanding their use of it, and then working with it—using it creatively in both this section and in the final speaking task.

Students learn useful structures for speaking in the **GRAMMAR** section, which offers a concise presentation and targeted practice. Vocabulary items are recycled here, providing multiple exposures leading to mastery. For additional practice with the grammar presented, students and teachers can consult the GRAMMAR BOOK REFERENCES at the end of the book for corresponding material in the *Focus on Grammar* and Azar series.

---

③ FOCUS ON SPEAKING

A VOCABULARY

◀ REVIEW

Read the radio advertisement and look at the picture on page 33. Fill in the blanks with the words from the box.

advice	famous	recycled	trendy
environment	material	trash	unusual

Do you want to enjoy camping and outdoor sports all year—even in the winter, in the rain? Then here's my _____ for you: You should wear Polar Fleece
1.
sports clothing. Polar Fleece clothing keeps you dry in wet weather and warm in cold weather. How is Polar Fleece made? Believe it or not, Polar Fleece clothing is made out of _____ plastic bottles! Recycled bottles go to a big
2.
factory¹. Machines at the factory clean the bottles, cut them into small pieces, and heat them. The bottles melt and become a liquid, like water. Then, another machine changes the liquid into a _____ that looks like wool. This "wool" is
3.
called Polar Fleece! This _____ material is comfortable and very warm. You can
4.
buy Polar Fleece winter clothes in many styles, so you will always look _____ !
5.
Polar Fleece also reduces _____ because it is made out of recycled plastic bottles.
6.
So it helps the _____ . Today, the name Polar Fleece is _____ all over
7.   8.
the world.

A skier wearing Polar Fleece

¹**factory:** a place where things are made with machines

32   UNIT 2

B GRAMMAR: Present and Past Tense of *Be*

1 *Read the excerpts. Follow the directions.*

NINA:	My name is Nina Rodriguez, and I'm interested in the Friendship Force.

RICK:	Language isn't so important.

ANNIE:	My group was great! We were all from the U.S., but we were very different. If you're in high school, go on the Experiment!

1. Underline all the present forms of *be*. Circle all the past forms of *be*.
2. What **negative** forms of *be* can you find? _____

PRESENT AND PAST TENSE OF *BE*	
1. The present tense of *be* has three forms: *am* *is* *are* To form negative statements, use *am, is, are + not.*	I **am** Nina. It **is** a friendship organization. You **are** my friend. We **are** friends. They **are** friends. They **are not** friends. He **is** my friend. He **is not** my friend. She **is** my friend. She **is not** my friend.
2. Contractions are short forms. Use contractions in speaking and in informal writing.	**I'm** Nina. **It's** a friendship organization. **You're** my friend. **We're** friends. **They're** friends. **He's** my friend. **She's** my friend.

Faraway Friends   15

The **PRONUNCIATION** section presents both controlled and freer, communicative practice of the sounds and patterns of English. Models from the listening selections reinforce content and vocabulary. This is followed by the **FUNCTION** section where students are exposed to functional language that prepares them to express ideas on a higher level. Examples have been chosen based on frequency, variety, and usefulness for the final speaking task.

The **PRODUCTION** section gives students an opportunity to integrate the ideas, vocabulary, grammar, pronunciation, and function presented in the unit. This final speaking task is the culminating activity of the unit and gets students to exchange ideas and express opinions in sustained speaking contexts. Activities are presented in a sequence that builds confidence and fluency, and allows for more than one "try" at expression. When appropriate, students practice some presentation skills: audience analysis, organization, eye contact, or use of visuals.

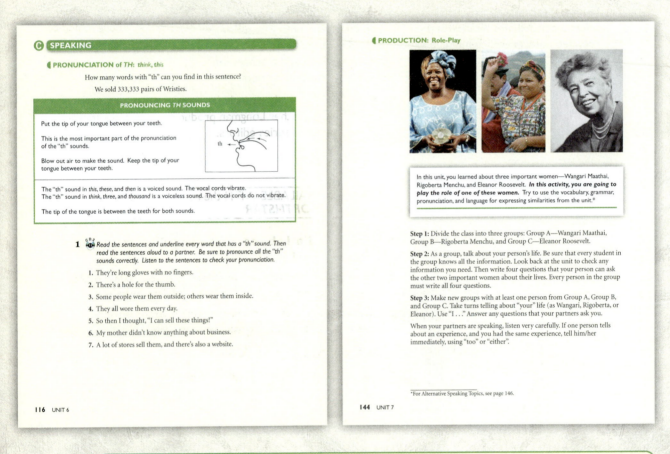

C SPEAKING

PRONUNCIATION of TH: think, this

How many words with "th" can you find in this sentence?

We sold 333,333 pairs of Wristies.

PRONOUNCING TH SOUNDS

Put the tip of your tongue between your teeth.

This is the most important part of the pronunciation of the "th" sounds.

Blow out air to make the sound. Keep the tip of your tongue between your teeth.

The "th" sound in *this*, *these*, and *then* is a voiced sound. The vocal cords vibrate.
The "th" sound in *think*, *three*, and *thousand* is a voiceless sound. The vocal cords do not vibrate.

The tip of the tongue is between the teeth for both sounds.

1 *Read the sentences and underline every word that has a "th" sound. Then read the sentences aloud to a partner. Be sure to pronounce all the "th" sounds correctly. Listen to the sentences to check your pronunciation.*

1. They're long gloves with no fingers.
2. There's a hole for the thumb.
3. Some people wear them outside; others wear them inside.
4. They all wore them every day.
5. So then I thought, "I can sell these things!"
6. My mother didn't know anything about business.
7. A lot of stores sell them, and there's also a website.

PRODUCTION: Role-Play

In this unit, you learned about three important women—Wangari Maathai, Rigoberta Menchu, and Eleanor Roosevelt. *In this activity, you are going to play the role of one of these women.* Try to use the vocabulary, grammar, pronunciation, and language for expressing similarities from the unit.*

Step 1: Divide the class into three groups: Group A—Wangari Maathai, Group B—Rigoberta Menchu, and Group C—Eleanor Roosevelt.

Step 2: As a group, talk about your person's life. Be sure that every student in the group knows all the information. Look back at the unit to check any information you need. Then write four questions that your person can ask the other two important women about their lives. Every person in the group must write all four questions.

Step 3: Make new groups with at least one person from Group A, Group B, and Group C. Take turns telling about "your" life (as Wangari, Rigoberta, or Eleanor). Use "I . . ." Answer any questions that your partners ask you.

When your partners are speaking, listen very carefully. If one person tells about an experience, and you had the same experience, tell him/her immediately, using "too" or "either".

*For Alternative Speaking Topics, see page 146.

ALTERNATIVE SPEAKING TOPICS are provided at the end of the unit. They can be used as *alternatives* to the final speaking task, or as *additional* assignments. RESEARCH TOPICS tied to the theme of the unit are organized in a special section at the back of the book.

COMPONENTS

TEACHER'S MANUAL WITH ACHIEVEMENT TESTS

Each level and strand of *NorthStar* has an accompanying Teacher's Manual with step-by-step **teaching suggestions**, including unique guidance for using *NorthStar* in secondary classes. The manuals include time guidelines, expansion activities, and techniques and instructions for using MyNorthStarLab. Also included are reproducible unit-by-unit achievement **tests** of **receptive** and **productive** skills, **answer keys** to both the student book and tests, and a unit-by-unit **vocabulary** list.

DVD

The *NorthStar* DVD has **engaging**, **authentic video clips**, including animation, documentaries, interviews, and biographies, that correspond to the themes in *NorthStar*. Each theme contains a three- to five-minute segment that can be used with either the *Reading and Writing* strand or the *Listening and Speaking* strand. The video clips can also be viewed in MyNorthStarLab.

COMPANION WEBSITE

The companion website, www.longman.com/northstar, includes resources for teachers, such as the **scope and sequence**, **correlations** to other Longman products and to state standards, and **podcasts** from the *NorthStar* authors and series editors.

MyNorthStarLab

PEARSON LONGMAN **mynorthstarlab**	AVAILABLE WITH the new edition of ***NORTHSTAR***

NorthStar is now available with **MyNorthStarLab**—an easy-to-use **online** program **for students and teachers** that saves time and improves results.

- ➤ **STUDENTS** receive **personalized instruction** and **practice** in all four skills. Audio, video, and test preparation are all in **one** place—available **anywhere, anytime**.
- ➤ **TEACHERS** can take advantage of many resources including online **assessments**, a flexible **gradebook**, and **tools for monitoring student progress**.

CHECK IT OUT! GO TO www.mynorthstarlab.com FOR A PREVIEW!

TURN THE PAGE TO SEE KEY FEATURES OF **MyNorthStarLab**.

MyNorthStarLab

MyNorthStarLab supports students with **individualized instruction**, **feedback**, and **extra help**. A wide array of resources, including a flexible **gradebook**, helps teachers manage student progress.

The MyNorthStarLab **WELCOME** page **organizes assignments and grades**, and **facilitates communication** between students and teachers.

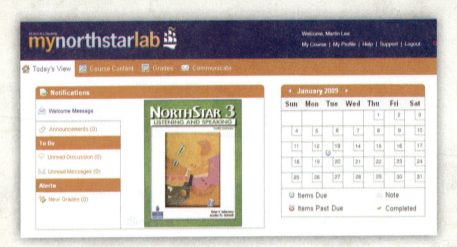

For each unit, MyNorthStarLab provides a **READINESS CHECK**.

➤ Activities **assess** student knowledge **before** beginning the unit and **follow up** with individualized instruction.

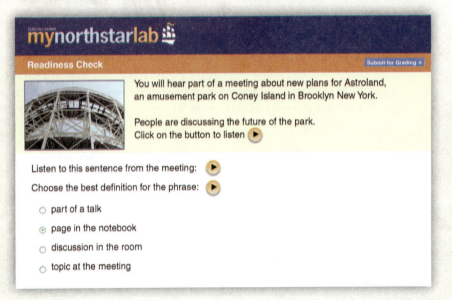

Student book material and **new** practice activities are available to students online.

➤ Students benefit from virtually unlimited **practice anywhere, anytime**.

Interaction with **Internet** and **video** materials will:

➤ Expand students' knowledge of the topic.

➤ Help students practice new vocabulary and grammar.

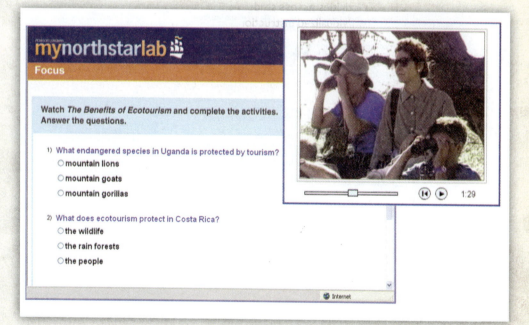

INTEGRATED SKILL ACTIVITIES in MyNorthStarLab challenge students to bring together the **language skills** and **critical thinking skills** that they have practiced throughout the unit.

mynorthstarlab

Integrated Task - Read, Listen, Write

Submit for Grading ▶

THE ADVENTURE OF A LIFETIME

We at the Antarctic Travel Society <u>encourage</u> you to consider an exciting guided tour of Antarctica for your next vacation.

The Antarctic Travel society carefully plans and operates tours of the Antarctic by ship. There are three trips per day leaving from <u>ports</u> in South America and Australia. Each ship carries only about 100 passengers at a time. Tours run from November through March to the ice-free areas along the coast of Antarctica.

In addition to touring the coast, our ships stop for on-land visits, which generally last for about three hours. Activities include guided sightseeing, mountain climbing, camping, <u>kayaking</u>, and <u>scuba diving</u>. For a longer stay, camping trips can also be arranged.

Our tours will give you an opportunity to experience the richness of Antarctica, including its wildlife, history, active research stations, and, most of all, its natural beauty.

Tours are <u>supervised</u> by the ship's staff. The staff generally includes <u>experts</u> in animal and sea life and other Antarctica specialists. There is generally one staff member for every 10 to 20 passengers. Theses trained and responsible individuals will help to make your visit to Antarctica safe, educational, and <u>unforgettable</u>.

READ, LISTEN AND WRITE ABOUT TOURISM IN ANTARCTICA
Read.
Read the text. Then answer the question.

According to the text, how can tourism benefit the Antartic?

▶ **Listen.**
Click on the Play button and listen to the passage.
Use the outline to take notes as you listen.

Main idea:

Seven things that scientists study:

The effects of tourism:

Write.
Write about the potential and risks in Antarctica.
Follow the steps to prepare.

Step 1
• Review the text and your outline from the listening task.
• Write notes about the benefits and risks of tourism.

Step 2
Write for 20 minutes. Leave 5 minutes to edit your work.

The MyNorthStarLab **ASSESSMENT** tools allow instructors to customize and deliver achievement tests online.

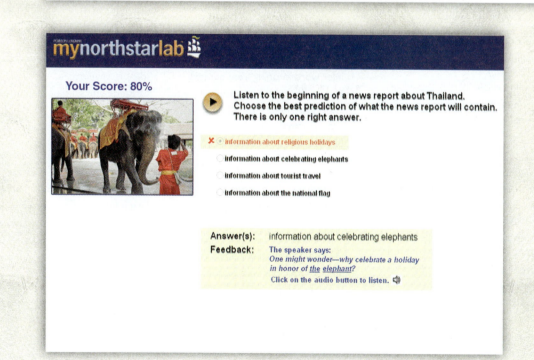

SCOPE AND SEQUENCE

UNIT	CRITICAL THINKING	LISTENING
Faraway Friends (1) **Theme:** Friendship **Listening One:** *Hello. This is the Friendship Force.* A conversation **Listening Two:** *The Best Summer of My Life!* An interview	Interpret a photograph Infer word meaning from context Differentiate between main ideas and details Relate the listenings to personal opinions and experiences Classify information	Predict content Identify main ideas Listen for details Infer information not explicit in the listening Listen to an interview Organize and synthesize information from the listenings Listen for rhythm in sentences
Recycled Fashion (2) **Theme:** Fashion **Listening One:** *Eco-Fashion* An interview **Listening Two:** *The Quilts of Gee's Bend* A radio broadcast	Interpret pictures Evaluate trends and preferences Infer word meaning from context Differentiate between main ideas and details Rate and evaluate personal preferences Classify information	Predict content Listen for main ideas Listen for details Interpret speakers' tone and attitude Complete an outline Organize and synthesize information from the listenings Listen for word stress Listen and evaluate student presentations
Rap Music (3) **Theme:** The arts **Listening One:** *A Famous Rapper: Tupac Shakur* An interview **Listening Two:** *Rap—Good or Bad?* A conversation	Analyze and label a picture Activate prior knowledge Relate listenings to personal values Infer information not explicit in the listening Infer word meaning from context Evaluate negative and positive aspects of rap music Classify information Express likes and dislikes	Predict content Listen for main ideas and correct false statements Listen for details Infer speakers' opinions and attitudes Identify opinions Organize and synthesize information from the listenings Classify sounds Listen to student interviews
Something Valuable (4) **Theme:** Special possessions **Listening One:** *The Hope Diamond* An excerpt from a museum tour **Listening Two:** *The Four Cs* A radio advertisement	Interpret a photograph Categorize information Infer word meaning from context Infer information not explicit in the listening Hypothesize another's point of view Support opinions with reasons Problem solve Reach a consensus	Predict content Place main ideas in sequential order Listen for supporting details Infer speakers' feelings and attitudes Listen to an advertisement Organize and synthesize information from the listenings Listen to role plays

SPEAKING	VOCABULARY	GRAMMAR	PRONUNCIATION
Share experiences Express opinions Interview classmates Practice the correct rhythm of sentences Ask for more information Practice introductions	Use context clues to find meaning Define words Use adjectives	Present and past tense of *be*	Rhythm
Share opinions Agree and disagree with statements Role-play Practice the correct word stress Use expressions for checking understanding Prepare a presentation	Use context clues to find meaning Use new words to complete sentences Use idiomatic expressions	Present progressive	Syllables and word stress
Ask and answer questions Express opinions about rap music Role-play Share personal opinions and knowledge about music Practice pronouncing vowel sounds Use appropriate language for expressing opinions Conduct an interview	Use context clues to find meaning Define words Classify expressions of like and dislike	Simple present tense with non-action (stative) verbs	/ɪ/ and /iy/
Share opinions and experiences Ask and answer questions Agree and disagree with statements Make suggestions Role-play a conversation	Use context clues to find meaning Use new vocabulary to complete a conversation Use idiomatic expressions	The simple present	-s endings for present tense

SCOPE AND SEQUENCE

UNIT	CRITICAL THINKING	LISTENING
5 **Together Is Better** **Theme:** Strength in numbers **Listening One:** *I Remember* A conversation **Listening Two:** *Elsa's Story* A narrative	Interpret the title of the unit Describe a photograph Recall information Activate prior knowledge Infer word meaning from context Infer information not explicit in the listening Hypothesize outcomes Evaluate issues related to Alzheimer's disease Rank personal preferences	Predict content Listen for main ideas Identify supporting details Infer speakers' opinions Listen to a narrative Organize and synthesize information from the listenings Classify sounds Listen to and evaluate student presentations
6 **Thinking Young: Creativity in Business** **Theme:** Business **Listening One:** *K-K Gregory, Young and Creative* A lecture **Listening Two:** *A Business Class* A lecture	Interpret pictures Infer word meaning from context Infer information not explicit in the listening Evaluate business initiatives Hypothesize another's point of view Reach a consensus Support opinions with reasons	Make predictions Listen for main ideas and correct false statements Listen for details Interpret people's opinions and attitudes Listen to a lecture Organize and synthesize information from the listenings
7 **Planting Trees for Peace** **Theme:** Famous people **Listening One:** *Wangari Maathai and the Green Belt* An excerpt from a TV show **Listening Two:** *Rigoberta Menchu, a Mayan Leader* A conversation	Analyze and label an illustration Activate prior knowledge Infer word meaning from context Analyze social issues Infer information not explicit in the listening Classify information Hypothesize another's point of view Relate information from the listenings to personal experience	Predict content Arrange events in chronological order Listen for details Infer speakers' opinions and attitudes Correct false statements Organize and synthesize information from the listenings

SPEAKING	VOCABULARY	GRAMMAR	PRONUNCIATION
Express opinions Share personal experiences Express personal preferences Interview a classmate Practice interrupting politely to ask a question Make a poster presentation	Use context clues to find meaning Define words Use idiomatic expressions	*Like to, want to, need to*	/ey/ and /ɛ/
Share opinions Agree and disagree with statements Create a conversation Interview a classmate React to information Role-play a business meeting	Use context clues to find meaning Define words Use idiomatic expressions	*There is / There are, There was / There were*	Pronunciation of *TH: think, this*
Express opinions Create a conversation Ask and answer questions Produce correct pronunciation of *-ed* endings Express similarities Perform a role play	Use context clues to find meaning Define words Use idiomatic expressions	Simple past tense	*-ed* endings

SCOPE AND SEQUENCE

UNIT	CRITICAL THINKING	LISTENING

8 **Driving You Crazy**
 	
Theme: Driving problems
Listening One: *Road Rage*
  A traffic school class
Listening Two: *Driving Phobia*
  A conversation
	Interpret a photograph
	Identify common driving problems
	Infer word meaning from context
	Propose solutions
	Support opinions with reasons
	Infer information not explicit in the listening
	Classify information
	Hypothesize another's point of view
	Analyze facts and agree on appropriate punishment
	Interpret a graph
		Predict feelings
		Listen for main ideas
		Identify supporting details
		Infer speakers' attitudes, opinions, and feelings
		Listen to a conversation
		Organize and synthesize information from the listenings
		Identify thought groups

9 **Only Child—Lonely Child?**
 	
Theme: Family
Listening One: *Changing Families*
  A TV talk show
Listening Two: *How Do Only Kids Feel?*
  A TV talk show
	Interpret illustrations
	Conduct a survey
	Infer word meaning from context
	Compare families
	Identify advantages and disadvantages
	Infer information not explicit in the listening
	Hypothesize another's point of view
	Propose solutions
	Interpret a graph
		Predict content
		Listen for main ideas
		Listen for details
		Correct false statements
		Infer speakers' opinions and attitudes
		Organize and synthesize information from the listenings
		Listen to student presentations

10 **The Beautiful Game**
 	
Theme: Sports
Listening One: *The Sports File*
  A radio show
Listening Two: *America Talks*
  A radio call-in show
	Interpret photographs
	Conduct a survey
	Activate prior knowledge
	Infer word meaning from context
	Infer information not explicit in the listening
	Rate preferences
	Classify information
	Support opinions with reasons
	Determine the meaning of a message
		Predict content
		Identify main ideas
		Identify details
		Infer speakers' intentions and attitudes
		Correct false statements
		Organize and synthesize information from the listenings
		Listen for important words
		Listen to and rate student presentations

SPEAKING	VOCABULARY	GRAMMAR	PRONUNCIATION
Share personal stories Agree and disagree with statements Role-play a scripted conversation Discuss experiences Break sentences into thought groups Express different points of view Discuss a case study and present a decision	Use context clues to find meaning Identify synonyms Use idiomatic expressions	Simple past and past progressive	Thought groups
Ask and answer questions Share experiences Express opinions Agree and disagree with statements Act out a scripted conversation Discuss ideas Create a role play	Use context clues to find meaning Define words Use idiomatic expressions	The future with *be going to*	"Going to" vs. "Gonna"
Share experiences Express opinions about sports Ask and answer questions Agree and disagree with statements Talk about sports Practice stressing important words Introduce reasons Create and present a TV ad	Use context clues to find meaning Define words Categorize vocabulary Use idiomatic expressions	*Should* for ideas and opinions	Stress on important words

ACKNOWLEDGMENTS

Many people contributed to this book, and I would like to acknowledge all of them. First of all, the *NorthStar* series exists because of the creative vision of Frances Boyd and Carol Numrich. I am very grateful to them for inviting me to contribute to this series.

Frances Boyd edited the original manuscript and offered ideas and support throughout the writing process. I thank her for all of her valuable contributions to the text. Debbie Sistino is the editor that every author dreams of. She guided this book from original manuscript to publication of the first edition with incredible dedication and good humor, and supervised production of the second edition with great talent and professionalism. I am especially grateful for the great respect she has for the classroom teacher's point of view. For guiding this text through its second edition, I am very grateful to my development editor, Dana Klinek. Dana made many valuable editorial contributions, and she was unfailingly patient and professional, even under the pressure of tight deadlines. Thanks also to Christine Cervoni and Robert Ruvo for their production expertise.

For getting me started on my professional journey, I would like to acknowledge John Fanselow, whose ideas about teaching and learning have guided me. And to my wonderful colleagues at Columbia University's ALP, from whom I have been learning for over 30 years: Thank you for keeping the journey so challenging, so rewarding, and so much fun! You have enriched my life immeasurably.

Finally, and most importantly, for allowing me to share their real stories, I am extremely grateful to Dr. Alan Dienstag, K-K Gregory, Professor Michael Ray, and Andy Stefanovich. Thanks too to Eli Escobar of WKCR, for educating me about hip-hop.

—Polly Merdinger

Reviewers

For the comments and insights they graciously offered to help shape the direction of the new edition of *NorthStar,* the publisher would like to thank the following reviewers and institutions.

Gail August, Hostos Community College; **Anne Bachmann**, Clackamas Community College; **Aegina Barnes**, York College, CUNY; **Dr. Sabri Bebawi**, San Jose Community College; **Kristina Beckman**, John Jay College; **Jeff Bellucci**, Kaplan Boston; **Nathan Blesse**, Human International Academy; **Alan Brandman**, Queens College; **Laila Cadavona-Dellapasqua**, Kaplan; **Amy Cain**, Kaplan; **Nigel Caplan**, Michigan State University; **Alzira Carvalho**, Human International Academy, San Diego; **Chao-Hsun (Richard) Cheng**, Wenzao Ursuline College of Languages; **Mu-hua (Yolanda) Chi**, Wenzao Ursuline College of Languages; **Liane Cismowski**, Olympic High School; **Shauna Croft**, MESLS; **Misty Crooks**, Kaplan; **Amanda De Loera**, Kaplan English Programs; **Jennifer Dobbins**, New England School of English; **Luis Dominguez**, Angloamericano; **Luydmila Drgaushanskaya**, ASA College; **Dilip Dutt**, Roxbury Community College; **Christie Evenson**, Chung Dahm Institute; **Patricia Frenz-Belkin**, Hostos Community College, CUNY; **Christiane Galvani**, Texas Southern University; **Joanna Ghosh**, University of Pennsylvania; **Cristina Gomes**, Kaplan Test Prep; **Kristen Grinager**, Lincoln High School; **Janet Harclerode**, Santa Monica College; **Carrell Harden**, HCCS, Gulfton Campus; **Connie Harney**, Antelope Valley College; **Ann Hilborn**, ESL Consultant in Houston; **Barbara Hockman**, City College of San Francisco; **Margaret Hodgson**, NorQuest College; **Paul Hong**, Chung Dahm Institute; **Wonki Hong**, Chung Dahm Institute; **John House**, Iowa State University; **Polly Howlett**, Saint Michael's College; **Arthur Hui**, Fullerton College; **Nina Ito**, CSU, Long Beach; **Scott Jenison**, Antelope Valley College; **Hyunsook Jeong**, Keimyung University; **Mandy Kama**, Georgetown University; **Dale Kim**, Chung Dahm Institute; **Taeyoung Kim**, Keimyung University; **Woo-hyung Kim**, Keimyung University; **Young Kim**, Chung Dahm Language Institute; **Yu-kyung Kim**, Sunchon National University; **John Kostovich**, Miami Dade College; **Albert Kowun**, Fairfax, VA; **David Krise**, Michigan State University; **Cheri (Young Hee) Lee**, ReadingTownUSA English Language Institute; **Eun-Kyung Lee**, Chung Dahm Institute; **Sang Hyock Lee**, Keimyung University; **Debra Levitt**, SMC; **Karen Lewis**, Somerville, MA; **Chia-Hui Liu**, Wenzao Ursuline College of Languages; **Gennell Lockwood**, Seattle, WA; **Javier Lopez Anguiano**, Colegio Anglo Mexicano de Coyoacan; **Mary March**, Shoreline Community College; **Susan Matson**, ELS Language Centers; **Ralph McClain**, Embassy CES Boston; **Veronica McCormack**, Roxbury Community College; **Jennifer McCoy**, Kaplan; **Joseph McHugh**, Kaplan; **Cynthia McKeag Tsukamoto**, Oakton Community College; **Paola Medina**, Texas Southern University; **Christine Kyung-ah Moon**, Seoul, Korea; **Margaret Moore**, North Seattle Community College; **Michelle Moore**, Madison English as a Second Language School; **David Motta**, Miami University; **Suzanne Munro**, Clackamas Community College; **Elena Nehrbecki**, Hudson County CC; **Kim Newcomer**, University of Washington; **Melody Nightingale**, Santa Monica College; **Patrick Northover**, Kaplan Test and Prep; **Sarah Oettle**, Kaplan, Sacramento; **Shirley Ono**, Oakton Community College; **Maria Estela Ortiz Torres**, C. Anglo Mexicano de Coyoac'an; **Suzanne Overstreet**, West Valley College; **Linda Ozarow**, West Orange High School; **Ileana Porges-West**, Miami Dade College, Hialeah Campus; **Megan Power**, ILCSA; **Alison Robertson**, Cypress College; **Ma. Del Carmen Romero**, Universidad del Valle de Mexico; **Nina Rosen**, Santa Rosa Junior College; **Daniellah Salario**, Kaplan; **Joel Samuels**, Kaplan New York City; **Babi Sarapata**, Columbia University ALP; **Donna Schaeffer**, University of Washington; **Lynn Schneider**, City College of San Francisco; **Errol Selkirk**, New School University; **Amity Shook**, Chung Dahm Institute; **Lynn Stafford-Yilmaz**, Bellevue Community College; **Lynne Ruelaine Stokes**, Michigan State University; **Henna Suh**, Chung Dahm Language Institute; **Sheri Summers**, Kaplan Test Prep; **Martha Sutter**, Kent State University; **Becky Tarver Chase**, MESLS; **Lisa Waite-Trago**, Michigan State University; **Carol Troy**, Da-Yeh University; **Luci Tyrell**, Embassy CES Fort Lauderdale; **Yong-Hee Uhm**, Myongii University; **Debra Un**, New York University; **José Vazquez**, The University of Texas Pan American; **Hollyahna Vettori**, Santa Rosa Junior College; **Susan Vik**, Boston University; **Sandy Wagner**, Fort Lauderdale High School; **Joanne Wan**, ASC English; **Pat Wiggins**, Clackamas Community College; **Heather Williams**, University of Pennsylvania; **Carol Wilson-Duffy**, Michigan State University; **Kailin Yang**, Kaohsing Medical University; **Ellen Yaniv**, Boston University; **Samantha Young**, Kaplan Boston; **Yu-san Yu**, National Sun Yat-sen University; **Ann Zaaijer**, West Orange High School

Faraway Friends

①FOCUS ON THE TOPIC

A PREDICT

Look at the picture. Discuss the questions with the class.

1. Read the title of the unit. What does it mean?

2. Are the people in the picture friends or family? Where are they?

3. Do you have friends from other countries? Where are they from?

I

B SHARE INFORMATION

1 *Did you ever visit or live in another country? Write your answers to the questions. Then ask a classmate the questions. Write his or her answers.*

	MY ANSWERS	MY CLASSMATE'S ANSWERS
1. Did you ever **visit** another country?	Yes / No	
a. (If NO, go to Question 2.) (If YES) What country did you **visit**?	I visited _____.	
b. Who did you go with? (alone, with my family, with my friends, with my school, with a tour group, other)	I went _____.	
c. Where did you stay? (at a hotel, at the home of friends / family, other)	I stayed _____.	
2. Did you ever **live** in a foreign country?	Yes / No	
a. (If NO, go to Question 3.) (If YES) What country did you **live** in?	I lived in _____.	
b. How long did you **live** there?	I lived there for _____.	

	MY ANSWERS	MY CLASSMATE'S ANSWERS
c. Who did you go with? (alone, with my family, with my friends, with my school, with a group, other)	I went _____.	
d. Who did you live with? (alone, at the home of friends / family, with a *host family*[1])	I lived _____.	
3. What countries do you want to visit?	I want to visit _____.	
4. What languages do you speak now?	I speak _____.	
5. What languages do you want to learn?	I want to learn _____.	

2 *Compare your answers with your classmates'.*

---

[1] **a host family:** also called a *homestay*, a family in a foreign country. You live with them and you learn about their life and their country.

A Friendship Force visitor with friends in Vietnam

Friendship Force Member Countries

Australia, Austria, Azerbaijan, Belarus, Belgium, Bosnia and Herzegovina, Brazil, Burundi, Canada, Cayman Islands, Chile, Colombia, Costa Rica, Croatia, Cyprus, Czech Republic, Egypt, Estonia, France, Georgia, Germany, Ghana, Hungary, India, Indonesia, Israel, Italy, Japan, Jordan, Kenya, Korea, Latvia, Mexico, Mongolia, Nepal, Netherlands, New Caledonia, New Zealand, Norway, Peru, Philippines, Poland, Romania, Russia, Singapore, Slovakia, South Africa, Sweden, Taiwan (ROC), Tanzania, Thailand, Turkey, Ukraine, United Kingdom, United States, Vietnam

1 *Look at the list of countries. Is there a Friendship Force club in your country?*

2 *Read and listen to the radio commercial for the Friendship Force.*

"A World of Friends Is a World of Peace."

And now, a message from the Friendship Force. They say, "A world of friends is a world of peace."

The Friendship Force is an **international** friendship organization. Friendship Force groups **travel** to foreign countries. In the new country, each Friendship Force visitor **stays** with a host family. The visitors **spend** a lot of time with their host families.

The visitors learn about their host family's life and **culture**. They become good friends. Every year, Friendship Force visitors **make** 40,000 new **friends** in 56 different countries. We're **excited about** all of these new international friends because "a world of friends is a world of peace."

Are you **interested in** the Friendship Force? Please go to our website for more information. Send us an **application** so we can learn more about you. Remember, when you make international friends, you help to make international peace.

3 *Circle the correct answer to complete the sentence.*

The Friendship Force says, "When you have international friends, _____."

a. you bring peace to the world   **b.** you can be in the Friendship Force

4 *Match the underlined words on the left with the definitions on the right. Write the numbers on the correct lines.*

1. With the Friendship Force, you can make <u>international</u> friends.

2. Friendship Force visitors <u>travel</u> to foreign countries.

3. Friendship Force visitors <u>stay</u> in a foreign family's home.

4. The visitors and their host families do many things together. They <u>spend</u> time together every day.

5. Host families teach their visitors about their <u>culture</u>, for example, their holidays, food, etc.

6. Friendship Force visitors like to <u>make friends</u> in foreign countries.

7. I really want to visit different countries. <u>I'm excited about</u> going to Europe.

8. I like to read books about Japan and talk to Japanese people. I'm <u>interested in</u> Japan.

9. Write all your information on your <u>application</u> to the Friendship Force: your name, address, e-mail, phone number, etc.

_____ **a.** get to know new people

_____ **b.** paper with information about yourself

_____ **c.** pass (time)

_____ **d.** feel eager and happy about

_____ **e.** go on a trip; go to a different place

_____ **f.** from many countries

_____ **g.** live in one place for a short time

_____ **h.** customs

_____ **i.** want more information about

2 FOCUS ON LISTENING

A   LISTENING ONE: Hello. This is the Friendship Force.

Nina and Rick are talking about the Friendship Force. Listen to the beginning of the conversation. Then answer the questions.

1. What are you listening to? Check (✔) the answer.

   ___✔___ a telephone call   _____ a radio talk show

2. What will Nina and Rick talk about? Check (✔) your ideas.

   ___✔___ host families   _____ shopping   ___✔___ traveling

   _____ hotels   _____ music   ___✔___ groups

   _____ students   _____ children   _____ languages

LISTEN FOR MAIN IDEAS

1 *Listen to the conversation between Nina and Rick. Read the sentences. Write **T** (true) or **F** (false).*

_____ 1. Friendship Force visitors can be young or old.

_____ 2. Some Friendship Force visitors stay in hotels.

_____ 3. Nina wants to stay with a host family in Thailand.

_____ 4. All host families speak English.

_____ 5. Nina and Rick agree that it's good to have international friends.

2 *Go back to Section 2A, Question 2. Were your answers correct?*

LISTEN FOR DETAILS

Listen again. Circle the correct answer to complete each sentence.

1. Each group has _____ people.
   a. 13 to 50   b. 15 to 30

2. Friendship Force groups meet for the first time _____.
   a. before they travel   b. in the new country

3. Nina thinks that when you live with a host family, you learn _____.
   a. their language   b. about their country

4. Nina _____ Thai (the language of Thailand).
   a. speaks a little   b. doesn't speak

5. Friendship Force visitors stay with their host families for two ____.

    a. weeks   **b.** months

6. After they stay with their host family, many Friendship Force visitors travel ____.

    a. to a different country   **b.** in the same country

7. Nina will get an application for the Friendship Force ____.

    a. from Rick   **b.** on the Internet

◖ MAKE INFERENCES

Listen to the excerpts from Listening One. Circle the correct answer to complete each sentence.

◉6 Excerpt One

    1. Nina is probably a ____ student.

        a. high school   **b.** college

◉7 Excerpt Two

    2. Nina is probably a ____ person.

        a. nervous   **b.** friendly

◉8 Excerpt Three

    3. Nina doesn't speak Thai. She is asking Rick, "Will I ____?"

        a. have problems   **b.** learn the language

◉9 Excerpt Four

    4. "People, not places" means, "You learn more about a new country when you ____."

        a. meet the people   **b.** visit the important places

◖ EXPRESS OPINIONS

Discuss the questions with the class.

1. Do you think it's good to stay with a host family? Why or why not?

2. Do you need to speak the same language well to make friends with someone? Why or why not?

3. What are the best ways to learn about another country?

Experiment students help to paint
a school in Costa Rica

Annie Quinn is an American high school student. Last summer, she traveled to
Costa Rica with a group called the Experiment in International Living (EIL).

*Listen to the interview with Annie. Then read each sentence. Write **T** (true)
or **F** (false). Correct the false sentences.*

_____ 1. *Experiment* group students always come from one city.

_____ 2. Annie and her group spent a few days together in Costa Rica.

_____ 3. Annie loved the students in her group.

_____ 4. Annie's host family was very friendly.

_____ 5. Annie's real name is "Ana."

_____ 6. Annie's host family helped her to learn Spanish.

_____ 7. You don't always need words to show your feelings.

_____ 8. *Experiment* groups usually stay in a foreign country for four weeks.

_____ 9. *Experiment* groups go to 37 different countries.

_____ 10. All *Experiment* students take classes in a foreign language.

◀ STEP 1: Organize

Look back at the information from Listenings One and Two. Check (✓) the correct column(s) for each sentence. You may check both columns.

	FRIENDSHIP FORCE	EXPERIMENT IN INTERNATIONAL LIVING
1. Visitors know each other before they travel.	✓	
2. People of any age can be in the group.	✓	✓
3. Only high school students can be in the group.		✓
4. You can go with the group only in the summer.	✓	✓
5. You can go with the group all year.	✓	✓
6. The visitors stay with host families.	✓	✓
7. The visitors stay with host families for three, four, or five weeks.	✓	✓
8. There are many classes.	✓	✓
9. It's not necessary to speak the host family's language.	✓	✓
10. The host families do not always speak English.	✓	✓
11. Applications are on the website.	✓	✓

Judy is a 15-year-old student. She is studying Chinese. She wants to visit China so she can practice speaking Chinese. Judy is talking to her friend Mei about different groups.

Role-play. Work with a partner. Complete the conversation with information from Step 1: Organize.

JUDY: The Friendship Force and the Experiment in International Living are both great! How can I decide?

MEI: Well, let's see. In the Friendship Force, you meet everyone before you travel. Everyone is from the same city.

JUDY: That's nice, but it's not that important. I like meeting new people from different cities.

MEI: OK. The Experiment is only for . . .

JUDY: The Friendship Force . . .

MEI: . . .

JUDY: . . .

3 FOCUS ON SPEAKING

A VOCABULARY

REVIEW

1 *A parent calls the American Field Service (AFS), an international student exchange program. Complete the conversation with the vocabulary from the box.*

application	international	spend
culture	is interested in	stay
excited about	make friends	traveling

AFS: Hello, AFS. Amanda Chu speaking.

PARENT: Hi, I'm calling for information about your _____

1.

summer programs.

AFS: Yes, how can I help you?

PARENT: Well, my son _is interested in_ going to Argentina.
2.

AFS: OK. We have three groups that are _traveling_ to Argentina
3.
this summer.

PARENT: Oh, that's great. Do the students in each group always

stay together?
4.

AFS: No. For one week, the students are together in Buenos Aires, the

capital city. They study some Spanish, and they learn about

Argentinean _culture_.
5.

PARENT: That's a good idea.

AFS: Yes, and it also gives them time to _make friends_ with the
6.

other students, before they go to their Argentinean host families.

PARENT: How much time do they _spend_ with their host
7.
families?

AFS: They live with them for a month. And most students say it's the best

time of their lives.

PARENT: Wow, I think my son will be very _glad about_ AFS.
8.

AFS: That's wonderful. I can e-mail you the _application_ now.
9.

PARENT: Thank you! That's great.

2 CD 7
11 *Now listen to the conversation. Check your answers to Exercise 1.*

1 *Read the conversation and the adjectives in the box. The adjectives describe people's personalities. Each word is listed with its opposite.*

QUESTION: What's he like? / What's she like?
    This means: "What kind of personality does he / she have?"
    Or: "How can you describe him / her?"
ANSWER: He's / She's <u>(adjective)</u>.

friendly	shy
funny	serious
interesting	boring
hardworking	lazy
talkative	quiet
calm	nervous
happy	sad

1. Mila

2. Saranya

3. James, Kelly, and Shiro

4. Lakesha

5. The students in my Spanish class

2 *Annie is showing her parents pictures of her friends from her summer in Costa Rica. She is telling her parents about each person. Work with a partner. Look at the pictures. For each picture, complete the conversation on the next page using the adjectives from the box. Take turns.*

Example (Look at picture 1.)

PARENT: Who's that?

ANNIE: That's _____Mila_____.

PARENT: What's she like?

ANNIE: She's _____friendly_____.

◖ CREATE

1 **a.** *Choose three adjectives **about you**. Write them in the box.*
b. *Interview three classmates. Ask, "What are you like?" Write their answers in the box.*

I am:	_____ is:
	(classmate's name)
_____	_____
_____	_____
_____	_____
_____ is:	_____ is:
(classmate's name)	**(classmate's name)**
_____	_____
_____	_____
_____	_____

c. *Share your answers with the class. Tell about one classmate who is **similar to you** and one who is **different from you**.*

Example

SIMILAR: Kei and I are quiet.

DIFFERENT: I am shy, but Wafa isn't shy. She's friendly.

2 **a.** *Complete the first box with information about yourself.*
   b. *Interview three different classmates. Ask these questions:*

Do you like to travel or spend time at home?

What are you interested in?

What are you excited about?

Complete the sentences: I like to _____ travel / spend time at home _____. am interested in _____. am excited about _____.	_____ (classmate's name) likes to _____. is interested in _____. is excited about _____.
_____ (classmate's name) likes to _____. is interested in _____. is excited about _____.	_____ (classmate's name) likes to _____. is interested in _____. is excited about _____.

   c. *Tell the class one fact about you and one fact about one of your classmates.*

   Example

   I like to travel. Sam is interested in other cultures.

1 *Read the excerpts. Follow the directions.*

> **NINA:** My name is Nina Rodriguez, and I'm interested in the Friendship Force.

> **RICK:** Language isn't so important.

> **ANNIE:** My group was great! We were all from the U.S., but we were very different. If you're in high school, go on the Experiment!

1. Underline all the <u>present</u> forms of *be*. Circle all the (past) forms of *be*.

2. What **negative** forms of *be* can you find? _____

PRESENT AND PAST TENSE OF *BE*	
I. The present tense of *be* has three forms: *am* *is* *are*	I **am** Nina. It **is** a friendship organization. You **are** my friend. We **are** friends.
To form negative statements, use *am*, *is*, *are* + *not*.	They **are** friends. They **are not** friends. He **is** my friend. He **is not** my friend. She **is** my friend. She **is not** my friend.
2. Contractions are short forms. Use contractions in speaking and in informal writing.	**I'm** Nina. **It's** a friendship organization. **You're** my friend. **We're** friends. **They're** friends. **He's** my friend. **She's** my friend.

To form negative statements, use: **a.** the **contraction of (subject + be) + not**	**I'm not** from Costa Rica. **You're not** ... **We're not** ... **They're not** ... **He's not** ... **It's not** ...
b. subject + (be + n't)	(This form does not work with *I*.) **You aren't** from Costa Rica. **We aren't** ... **They aren't** ... **He isn't** ... **It isn't** ...
3. The past tense of *be* has two forms: *was* and *were*.	I **was** here yesterday. You **were** my friend.
4. To form negative statements, use *was / were* + *not* or the contractions *wasn't / weren't*.	I **was not (wasn't)** in class yesterday.
5. To form questions in the present and the past tense, use *be* + subject	**Is she** your friend? **Are you** friends now? **Where is your friend** now? **When were you** in Costa Rica?

2 *Complete the conversation with the correct form of **be**. Use contractions wherever possible. Then check your answers with a partner's. Read the conversation together.*

Friendship Force International
Building global goodwill through personal friendships

233 PEACHTREE ST NW • SUITE 2250 • ATLANTA, GA 30303 USA • PH 404.522.9490 • FAX 404.688.6148

Q: What kind of people does the Friendship Force look for?

A: Friendship Force visitors _____are_____ interested in other cultures. They
  1.
____aren't____ afraid of new places.
  2. (neg.)

Q: ____Is____ it necessary to speak another language?
  3.

A: No, it ____isn't____! Language ____is not____ a big problem for the visitors.
  4. (neg.)   **5. (neg.)**

Q: What if we have a problem when we ____are____ in another country?
  6.

A: Every Friendship Force group has a leader. The leader ____is____ always near
  7.
you. For example, last year, one visitor ____was____ sick in Germany. Her host
  8.
family called her Friendship Force leader. The leader took her to the doctor
immediately. Luckily, she ____wasn't____ very sick. The next day, she
  9. (neg.)
____was____ fine. So remember, when you travel with the Friendship Force, you
  10.
____are not____ alone.
  11. (neg.)

Q: I really want to travel with the Friendship Force, but I'm not ____ sure when I
  12. (neg.)
can go. Is that a problem?

A: No, that ____is not____ a problem. There ____are____ many different
  13. (neg.)   **14.**
groups every year. The schedule ____is____ on our website.
  15.

Friendship Force International
233 Peachtree St. NW (Suite 2250)
Atlanta, Georgia 30303 USA

◀ **PRONUNCIATION: Rhythm**

1 🔘 *Listen to the conversation.*

A: WHERE are you **FROM**?
B: I'm from **CHI**na. HOW about **YOU**?
A: COsta **RI**ca.

These sentences show the rhythm of English sentences. The words and syllables in capital letters are longer and louder than the other words and syllables. The last word in each sentence is the longest and loudest word. It tells the most important information.

2 🔘 *The rhythm at the beginning of each group of sentences shows the rhythm of the sentences. Listen to the rhythm and sentences and repeat them.*

1. Rhythm: DA da da **DA**

   a. THIS is my **FRIEND**.
   b. WHERE are you **FROM**?
   c. KEI'S from Ja**PAN**.
   d. HOW about **YOU**?
   e. WHERE do you **LIVE**?

2. Rhythm: da da **DA** da

   a. I'm a **STU**dent.
   b. He's from **CHI**na.
   c. She's a **DOC**tor.
   d. It's ex**CIT**ing.
   e. He's our **TEA**cher.

3. Rhythm: DA da **DA** da

   a. NICE to **MEET** you.
   b. THIS is **NI**na.
   c. WHAT'S the **PRO**blem?
   d. I'm a **STU**dent.
   e. WHAT's your **MA**jor?

4. Other rhythms.

   a. da **DA**   I'm **LEE**.   I'm **JOE**.   She's **KATE**.
   b. da **DA** da   She's **A**na.   I'm **HI**ro.   He's **CAR**los.
   c. da da **DA**   I'm in **CLASS**.   She's Ma**RIE**.   He's at **HOME**.

3 🔊 *Listen to the conversation and practice it with a partner.*

LILY: **HI.** I'm **LI**ly.
CARLOS: NICE to **MEET** you. I'm **CAR**los.
LILY: WHERE are you **FROM?**
CARLOS: **CO**sta **RI**ca. HOW about **YOU?**
LILY: I'm from **CHI**na.
CARLOS: WHAT do you **DO?**
LILY: I'm a **STU**dent. WHAT about **YOU?**

4 *Work with a partner. Complete the conversation with the sentences from the box. Then practice the conversation with your partner.*

> **a.** I'm from **TO**kyo. HOW about **YOU?**
> **b.** ~~NICE to **MEET** you. I'm **HI**ro.~~
> **c.** WHAT'S your **MA**jor?
> **d.** YES, I **AM.** HOW about **YOU?**

CARLOS: Hi, I'm **CAR**los.
HIRO: <u>Nice to meet you. I'm Hiro.</u>
CARLOS: Hi **HI**ro. WHERE are you **FROM?**
HIRO: _____
CARLOS: I'm from **CO**sta **RI**ca. Are you a **STU**dent?
HIRO: _____
CARLOS: I'm a **STU**dent, **TOO.**
HIRO: _____

◀ FUNCTION: Asking for More Information

Sometimes in a conversation, we want to ask someone for more information.

NINA: I'm interested in the Friendship Force,
but **I have some questions**.

INTERVIEWER: **Can you tell us about** your group?
I'd like to know more about your host family.

ANNIE: And I also learned that language is not always so important.
INTERVIEWER: **What do you mean?**

Here are some useful phrases for asking for more information.

I have a question / some questions.   I'd like to know more about (that).

Can you tell me more about (that)?   Can you explain why / how?

What do you mean?

Work with a partner. Student A, read a statement. Student B, ask for more information. Student A, give Student B more information. Use the information from this unit or your own ideas.

Example

A: It's important for high school students to live in a foreign country.
B: Can you explain why?
A: It's good to learn about another country. Living in a country is the best way to learn about it.

1. You can learn a lot when you travel.

2. With a friend, speaking the same language isn't really important.

3. The AFS program is really great!

4. Friendship Force groups are very special.

Switch roles.

5. Living with a host family is a great experience.

6. It's very important to speak two languages.

7. Some people are really nervous when they go to a foreign country.

8. A world of friends is a world of peace.

> **In this activity, you are going to introduce a friend to two of your classmates.** Try to use the vocabulary, grammar, pronunciation, and language for describing personalities and interests from the unit.*

Follow the steps.

Step 1: Work with a partner. Student A, ask Student B questions about his or her native country or city, native language, profession, or favorite subject, etc. Take notes on your partner's answers. Then switch roles.

Step 2: Find another pair of students (Students C and D). Student A, tell the pair four things about Student B. Students C and D, after each piece of information, ask questions for more information. Use the phrases from Function on page 20. Student B, answer the questions.

Step 3: Complete the activity three more times so that everyone in the group has a chance to tell about someone, ask questions, and answer questions.

Example

A: I'm going to tell you about my friend Francisco. He's new to our city.
C: What do you mean?
B: I moved here last week. I'm from Buenos Aires, Argentina.
A: Francisco speaks three languages.
D: That's interesting! I have a question. Francisco, what languages do you speak?
B: Spanish, Portuguese, and some English.
A: Francisco is studying history.
C: Cool. Can you tell me more about that?

---

*For Alternative Speaking Topics, see page 22.

ALTERNATIVE SPEAKING TOPICS

Discuss one of the topics. Use the vocabulary and grammar from the unit.

1. Do groups like the Friendship Force, EIL, and AFS really help bring peace to the world? Why or why not?

2. Which group are you interested in? Why?

RESEARCH TOPICS, see page 214.

Recycled Fashion

RECYCLE

① FOCUS ON THE TOPIC

Ⓐ PREDICT

Look at the pictures. Discuss the questions with the class.

1. What is happening?

2. What does *recycle* mean?

3. What does the title mean?

23

Walk around the room. Ask three classmates the questions. Check (✓) their answers.

1. Where do you usually get your clothes?

   Student 1: _____ at a store   _✓_ from other   _____ at home (I make
                                      people   my own clothes.)

   Student 2: _____ at a store   _____ from other   _✓_ at home (I make
                                      people   my own clothes.)

   Student 3: _✓_ at a store   _____ from other   _____ at home (I make
                                      people   my own clothes.)

2. What do you usually do with your old clothes?

   Student 1: _____ I keep them   _✓_ I give them   _____ I use them for
                                       away   something else

   Student 2: _____ I keep them   _✓_ I give them   _____ I use them for
                                       away   something else

   Student 3: _____ I keep them   _✓_ I give them   _____ I use them for
                                       away   something else

1 ᶜᴰ₇ *Read and listen to the radio show. Rina is calling for advice about what to do*
 ⑮ *with her old clothing.*

RINA: Hi, My name is Rina. I have a lot of old clothes. I don't wear
             them anymore. I don't want to put these clothes in the **trash**.
             Can you help? Do you have any **advice**?

RADIO HOST: You don't need to throw away your old clothes. There are many
             things you can do with old clothes:

             • you can give them to friends or younger people in your
               family.

             • you can sell them at garage sales[1].

             • you can give them to charity[2] (for example, Goodwill, the
               Salvation Army, and thrift stores)

             • or you can **recycle** your clothes.

_____

[1]**garage sale:** a sale of used clothes and other things at a person's house (usually in front of
 the garage)

[2]**charity:** an organization that gives money, food, or clothing to poor people

RINA: Really? Recycle clothing? How?

RADIO HOST: A lot of new fashion designers are using old clothes to make new clothing. One designer is Chrisi A. She has a website called Chrisi A. Designs. Chrisi A. uses old clothing to make wonderful new clothes.

RINA: That sounds great. I have an old silk shirt. Can I recycle it?

RADIO HOST: Yes! You can use the old silk material to make something new. Designers like Chrisi make clothes from different kinds of **materials**. Chrisi loves **organic** materials, silk . . . cotton . . . natural materials, not man-made.

RINA: But why does she make clothes out of recycled materials?

RADIO HOST: There are two reasons. First, she wants her clothes to be **unusual**, you know, different from other people's clothes. And second, using recycled materials reduces trash, and that helps the **environment**.

RINA: I see. That's a good idea. Do a lot of people wear recycled clothes?

RADIO HOST: Yes! Recycled clothes are becoming popular all around the world. A lot of **famous** people wear them. Recycled clothes are **trendy**!

2 *Match the words on the left with the definitions on the right.*

_____ 1. unusual   **a.** natural, made with no chemicals

_____ 2. recycle   **b.** a good idea; a suggestion about what to do

_____ 3. trash   **c.** very different

_____ 4. environment   **d.** use again in a different way

_____ 5. trendy   **e.** known by many people

_____ 6. famous   **f.** something you throw away

_____ 7. materials   **g.** the air, water, and land

_____ 8. organic   **h.** popular; many people do things this way

_____ 9. advice   **i.** cloths such as cotton or silk; people use them to make clothes

FOCUS ON LISTENING

A **LISTENING ONE: Eco-Fashion**

Eco-Fashion by Deborah Lindquist

CD 7
16 *Listen to the first part of the interview with fashion designer Deborah Lindquist. Then answer the questions.*

1. What is eco-fashion?

2. How is eco-fashion different?

3. What words will you probably hear in the next part of the interview? Check (✓) three.

_____ color

_____ music

_____ language

_____ stores

_____ pretty

_____ books

◀ LISTEN FOR MAIN IDEAS

1 🔘 *Now listen to the whole interview. Read the list. Check (✓) the main ideas.*

_____ 1. Eco-fashion uses new clothes.

_____ 2. Deborah Lindquist thinks vintage[1] materials are beautiful.

_____ 3. Eco-fashion is good for the environment.

_____ 4. Fashion design is a difficult job.

_____ 5. Deborah Lindquist says that people like to wear unusual clothes.

_____ 6. Not many stores sell eco-fashion.

2 *Go back to Section 2A, Question 3, on page 26. Were your answers correct?*

◀ LISTEN FOR DETAILS

🔘 *Listen to the interview again. Circle the correct answer to complete each sentence.*

1. Lindquist uses old clothing from _____ and Japan.
   a. England
   b. India

2. Lindquist thinks that more _____ need to help the environment.
   a. countries
   b. companies

3. _____ countries have eco-fashion companies.
   a. Several
   b. Many

4. Going to _____ is a good way to become a fashion designer.
   a. New York
   b. fashion school

5. Some of Lindquist's fashions have _____ characters.
   a. Korean
   b. Chinese

6. Lindquist gets new ideas for fashion every _____.
   a. year
   b. day

7. Eco-fashion is becoming _____.
   a. popular
   b. expensive

---
[1]**vintage:** old and showing high quality

Listen to the excerpts. Circle the best answer to complete each sentence.

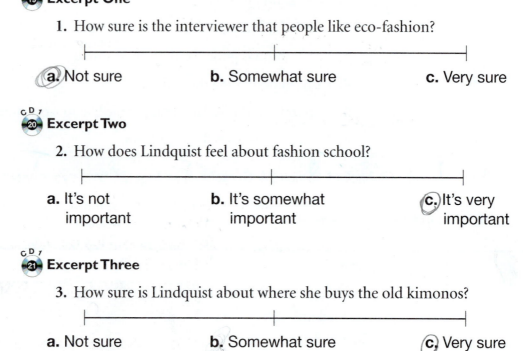

CD 7
19 Excerpt One

1. How sure is the interviewer that people like eco-fashion?

a. Not sure   **b.** Somewhat sure   **c.** Very sure

CD 7
20 Excerpt Two

2. How does Lindquist feel about fashion school?

a. It's not important   **b.** It's somewhat important   **c.** It's very important

CD 7
21 Excerpt Three

3. How sure is Lindquist about where she buys the old kimonos?

a. Not sure   **b.** Somewhat sure   **c.** Very sure

◀ **EXPRESS OPINIONS**

Read the statements. Do you agree or disagree? Check (✓) one. Then discuss your ideas with a partner.

1. I really like organic materials, especially cotton and silk. They are soft and beautiful.

   ✓ Agree

   _____ Disagree

2. Fashion is very important to me. I like to wear beautiful clothes.

   _____ Agree

   _____ Disagree

3. I want more companies to help the environment. I think more companies should make clothes with recycled materials.

   _____ Agree

   _____ Disagree

4. I don't like to spend money on clothing. I don't think it's necessary to spend a lot of money on pants or a dress.

_____ Agree

_____ Disagree

5. I want to be a fashion designer. I think making new clothes is very exciting.

_____ Agree

_____ Disagree

B LISTENING TWO: The Quilts of Gee's Bend

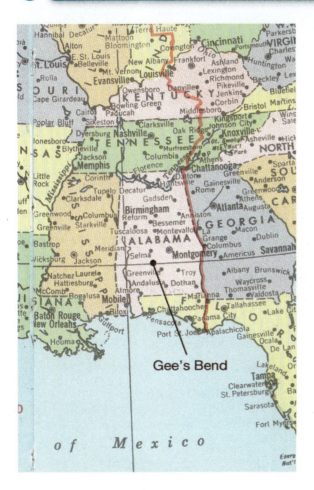

Gee's Bend

Gee's Bend is the name of a small town in Alabama. The women of Gee's Bend are famous for their quilts. They use old materials to make beautiful quilts.

Listen to the radio broadcast about the women in a town called Gee's Bend. Then complete the outline with the information you hear. Circle the correct answer.

A. What are the Gee's Bend quilts?

    1. Gee's Bend quilts are _____ made by hand.

        a. clothing
        b. blankets

    2. They are made out of old clothing such as jeans and _____.

        a. dresses
        b. sweaters

B. Why are they art?

    3. The women put all the _____ together carefully.

        a. colors
        b. pieces

    4. The quilts look beautiful and _____.

        a. unusual
        b. new

C. Why do they have special meaning?

    5. One woman made a quilt to remember her _____.

        a. mother
        b. husband

    6. _____, mothers, and daughters make them together.

        a. Neighbors
        b. Grandmothers

STEP 1: Organize

Answer the questions in the chart. Use information from Listenings One and Two.

USING RECYCLED MATERIALS		
	Deborah Lindquist	**Gee's Bend Women**
1. What do they do?	Makes trendy clothes with unusual materials; makes eco-fashion	*make clothing, remember events*
2. Why do they use recycled materials?	*They're economical, it's good for the environment*	*old materials don't cost any money*
3. Where do they live?	*(illegible handwriting)*	*Alabama*

STEP 2: Synthesize

Imagine that Deborah Lindquist from Listening One and the Gee's Bend woman from Listening Two are speaking to a news reporter.

1 *Role-play. Work in groups of three. Complete the conversation with information from Step 1: Organize.*

REPORTER:	What do you make?
LINDQUIST:	I make . . .
GEE'S BEND WOMAN:	Well, I don't make . . .
REPORTER:	Why do you use recycled materials?
GEE'S BEND WOMAN:	I use them because . . .
LINDQUIST:	I use recycled materials . . .

2 *Practice responding to the questions. Then share one question and the answer with the class.*

3 FOCUS ON SPEAKING

A VOCABULARY

◀ REVIEW

Read the radio advertisement and look at the picture on page 33. Fill in the blanks with the words from the box.

advice	famous	recycled	trendy
environment	material	trash	unusual

Do you want to enjoy camping and outdoor sports all year—even in the winter, in the rain? Then here's my

_____ for you: You should wear Polar Fleece
1.

sports clothing. Polar Fleece clothing keeps you dry in wet

weather and warm in cold weather. How is Polar Fleece made?

Believe it or not, Polar Fleece clothing is made out of

_____ plastic bottles! Recycled bottles go to a big
2.

factory[1]. Machines at the factory clean the bottles, cut them

into small pieces, and heat them. The bottles melt and become

a liquid, like water. Then, another machine changes the liquid

A skier wearing Polar Fleece

into a _____ that looks like wool. This "wool" is
3.

called Polar Fleece! This _____ material is comfortable and very warm. You can
4.

buy Polar Fleece winter clothes in many styles, so you will always look ___trendy___!
5.

Polar Fleece also reduces ___trash___ because it is made out of recycled plastic bottles.
6.

So it helps the _____. Today, the name Polar Fleece is ___famous___ all over
7.   8.

the world.

---

[1]**factory:** a place where things are made with machines

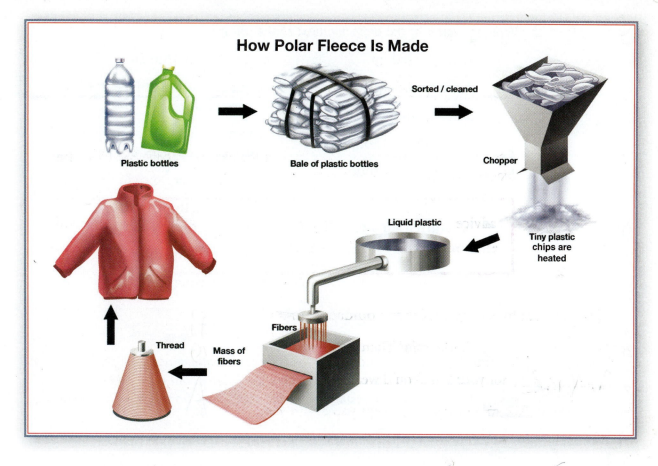

How Polar Fleece Is Made

Plastic bottles

Bale of plastic bottles

Sorted / cleaned

Chopper

Liquid plastic

Tiny plastic chips are heated

Fibers

Thread

Mass of fibers

◖ EXPAND

1 *Read the conversation with a partner. The boldfaced expressions are about clothes.*

LORI: Wow, you**'re** so **dressed up**!

MIRANDA: Yeah, I'm going to a big party tonight, so I'm wearing my new dress.

LORI: Well, **it looks great on you**! Where did you get it?

MIRANDA: I bought it on Chrisi A.'s website. She makes all of her clothes out of recycled materials.

LORI: Wow, a recycled dress. It's beautiful! And **it fits you perfectly**!

MIRANDA: Yeah, it's just the right size.

LORI: I can't buy clothes online. I need to **try** them **on** first.

MIRANDA: Well, I know my size. I always **wear a medium** in dresses. But if you buy something that **doesn't fit**, you can **return it for a refund**.

LORI: That's good. Can you help me find something nice on Chrisi A.'s website?

MIRANDA: Sure. Let's go shopping right now!

2 *Write the letter of the definition next to the phrase.*

_____ **1.** be dressed up

_____ **2.** (it) looks great on (you)

_____ **3.** it fits you perfectly

_____ **4.** try (them/it) on

_____ **5.** I wear a (medium)

_____ **6.** doesn't fit

_____ **7.** return it for a refund

a. it is exactly your size

b. put on clothing to see if it is the correct size

c. wearing formal or special clothes; not everyday clothing

d. you look very nice in this (clothing)

e. take something back to a store and get your money back

f. my size is (medium)

g. is the wrong size

◀ CREATE

1 *Work with a partner. Student A owns a recycled clothing and quilt store. Student B is a customer. The customer wants to know more about recycled clothing and quilts. Ask and answer questions. Use the vocabulary from Review and Expand.*

Example

STORE OWNER: Can I help you?
CUSTOMER: Yes, can you tell me more about recycled clothing?
STORE OWNER: Sure . . .

2 *Practice your conversation. Then share one question and answer with the class.*

B GRAMMAR: Present Progressive

1 *Look at the sentences. Underline the verbs.*

1. Eco-fashion is becoming trendy.

2. More and more stores are selling eco-fashion.

3. She's wearing a recycled kimono.

4. Why is she wearing old clothes?

2 *What are the two parts of the verb? How is the verb in Question 4 different?*

3 *Which sentences tell about an action right now / at this moment? Which sentences tell about a change that is happening these days (but not at this moment)?*

Use the present progresive to describe actions or situations that are happening (1) right now, at this moment, or (2) now, as in this month, this year, or these days.

PRESENT PROGRESSIVE	
1. To form the present progressive, use the **present tense of the *be* verb + the *-ing* form of the main verb.**	The model **is wearing** a recycled sari.
a. If the **main verb ends in -e,** drop the **-e** and add **-ing.**	The women of Gee's Bend **are making** beautiful quilts for their families.
b. The verb **get** has a consonant / vowel / consonant pattern. Double the final consonant before **-ing.** Similar verbs include *swim, begin, put,* and *run.*	Clothing **is getting** more expensive.
2. For negative sentences, use the **be verb + *not* + the main verb.**	They **are not wearing** pajamas. He **is not wearing** jeans.
3. For **yes / no** questions, put the **be verb before the subject.**	**Are** they **using** old materials?
4. For **wh-** questions, use the **question word(s) + be verb + subject + main verb.**	**Where is** she **working**? **What** material **are they using**?

4 *Complete the conversation with the present progressive form of the verbs in parentheses.*

A: What _____ are _____ you _____ doing _____?
                                          1. (do)

B: I _____ a TV show about Emmeline Child.
           2. (watch)

A: Who's Emmeline Child?

B: She's a fashion designer. She makes clothes out of recycled materials. She

_____ a jacket now.
     3. (make)

(continued on next page)

A: What kind of material _____ she _____?
                                                    4. (use)

B: She ___is making___ this jacket out of an old pair of jeans. Do you like
              5. (make)

what she ___wearing___?
              6. (wear)

A: Yeah, it's cool. Why?

B: She made it out of recycled clothing. Her clothes _____ very
                                                              7. (become)

popular these days.

5 *Work in pairs. Student A, look at the picture on this page. Student B, look at Student Activities page 207. Ask your partner **yes / no** questions about his or her picture. Then, answer questions about your picture. Try to find three or four differences between the pictures. Use the present progressive.*

Example

A: Do you have a picture of a woman?
B: No, a man.
A: Is he making something?
B: . . .
A: Is he _____ing . . . ?
B: . . .

C SPEAKING

PRONUNCIATION: Syllables and Word Stress

Syllables are parts of words. The word *woman* has two syllables. *Designer* has three syllables. *New* has one syllable.

1 CD1 23 *Listen to the boldfaced words in the conversation. How many syllables do the words have? Write the number of syllables over each word.*

A: What's in the **box**?
                                  ¹

B: Let's see . . . There's an old **jacket**, a **shirt**, a **quilt** and a . . . what's this? A **wedding** dress!

SYLLABLES AND WORD STRESS

1-syllable words	2-syllable words	3-syllable words
shirt	jacket	designer
quilt	wedding	beautiful

In words with two or more syllables, one syllable is stressed.

The stressed syllable is long and loud. Unstressed syllables are not long or loud.

w e dding   **j a** cket   **b e a u** tiful

---

2 CD1 24 *Listen to the words and repeat them. Then underline the syllables. Put a line over the stressed syllable. Then listen again and pronounce each word. Make the stressed syllables long.*

1. blan ket
2. scarf
3. garage
4. trash
5. clothes
6. popular
7. jeans

8. fashion
9. reason
10. agree
11. famous
12. expensive
13. brother
14. belt

15. decide
16. pocket
17. mother
18. student
19. recycle

3 CD1 25 *a. Listen to the sentences and repeat them. Then look at the boldfaced words. Put a line over the stressed syllable.*

1. Here's some **clothing**.

2. **Listen** to the **music**.

3. **Answer** the **question**.

4. Does it have a **pocket**?

(continued on next page)

5. Put this in the **garage**.

6. I can't **decide**.

7. I **agree**.

8. This is my **sister**.

9. That's good **advice**.

10. I don't **believe** you.

11. She **designs** hats.

12. Let's **invite** the other **students**.

13. Did you **visit** your **parents**?

14. I want to **study fashion**.

b. *Work with a partner and check the stressed syllables in part a. Then look at the boldfaced words and answer the questions below.*

1. Which words are nouns? Write them on the line.

   clothing, _____

2. Which words are verbs? Write them on the line.

   _____

3. Circle the best answer for the rules below.

   Rules for stressing two-syllable nouns and verbs:

   a. (Most / A few) two-syllables nouns are stressed on the first syllable.

   b. (Most / About half of) two-syllable verbs are stressed on the second syllable.

4 CD 7 *Listen to the conversations and write the words in the blanks. Then practice*
26 *the conversations with a partner.*

A and B found a box in A's garage.

A: What's in the box? Is that a wool _____?

B: Let's see . . . There's a _____, some _____ things, and . . . what's this?

A: A _____? Maybe a _____? I can't _____.

B: Let's keep it. The _____ is nice.

◀ FUNCTION: Checking for Understanding

1 *When we explain things to people, it is helpful to check their understanding. Read the explanation. An instructor is telling students how to wear a kimono. Look at the boldfaced expressions.*

INSTRUCTOR: Welcome to the World Clothing class. Today we're discussing the traditional dress of Japan, the kimono. Let's talk about how to put on the kimono. First, put on the white collar. **See?** It goes under the kimono. Then put on the kimono. That's the easy part. Next, put the right side of the kimono over your body, and then put the left side of the kimono over that. **Got it?** That's very important. **Any questions?**

STUDENT: Can you put the left side over your body?

INSTRUCTOR: No. You do that only when you dress a body for a funeral[1]. So, you never do that when you're getting dressed for a regular day. **Is that clear?** Now, the next part is the belt. You wear a special belt called an *obi*. You must wear the *obi* belt with the kimono. **OK?**

USEFUL EXPRESSIONS

See?	Got it?
Is that clear?	Does that make sense?
Any questions?	OK?

---

2 *Work in groups of four. Take turns explaining one of the choices. Use the expressions from the box to check for understanding.*

a. how to put on special clothing from your culture

b. how to put on a tie

c. how to dress for a sport

d. your own idea: _____

---

[1]**funeral:** a special ceremony for a person who has died

In this activity, imagine you are going to make something new out of old materials. Choose the materials, decide what to make, and draw a picture of your new design. Then present your design to the class. Explain how to make it. Try to use the vocabulary, grammar, pronunciation, and language for checking for understanding from the unit.*

Follow the steps.

Step 1: Work with a partner. Choose two or more of the materials.

a. a kimono

b. a sari

c. an old pair of jeans

d. a quilt

e. a baseball cap

f. a leather jacket

g. an old pair of gloves

h. a wedding dress

i. a silk scarf

j. your own idea: _____

Step 2: Discuss how you can use the materials to make something new. You can make a new piece of clothing or something to use or look at.

Step 3: Draw a picture of your design. Show your picture to the class and explain your design.

Draw your new design here:

Step 4: Listen to your classmates and ask questions about their designs.

*For Alternative Speaking Topics, see page 42.

Example Presentation

We chose an old pair of jeans.

We recycled the old pair of jeans to make a jeans bag. You can use it to carry books, your wallet, and your cell phone. This is how you make the bag.

First, you cut off the legs of the jeans.

a sewing machine

Then you sew the bottom together.

Next, take a piece of the leg of the jeans to make a strap. Sew the strap to the top of the bag.

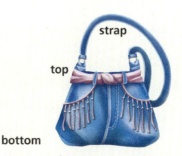

strap

top

bottom

Now you have a trendy jeans bag. See? Is that clear? Any questions?

ALTERNATIVE SPEAKING TOPICS

Discuss one of the topics. Use the vocabulary and grammar from the unit.

1. Imagine that you have a new baby. A friend gives you a baby gift. It is a beautiful quilt made out of recycled cotton clothing. Will you use this quilt for your baby? Why or why not? Check (✓) the answer that you agree with. Explain your reason.

   _____ **1.** No, I will not use the quilt.

   _____ **2.** Maybe I will use the quilt. It depends . . .

   _____ **3.** Yes, I will use the quilt.

   Now discuss your ideas in a small group.

2. A quilt is an example of **folk art**. This is art made by the people of a country. It is not made by famous artists. Look at some other examples of folk art:

   a. rugs made out of old clothes

   b. dolls made out of corn husks

c. mats made out of rice leaves

d. rattles (musical instruments) made out of dry gourds (vegetables)

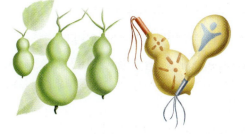

Now discuss the questions.

1. What kind of folk art do people make in your home culture?

2. Can you make any folk art? Would you like to learn how?

RESEARCH TOPICS, see page 215.

Rap Music

1. _____

2. _____

3. _____

4. _____

5. _____

① FOCUS ON THE TOPIC

Ⓐ PREDICT

1 *Look at the picture. Write each word on the line next to the person or thing it describes.*

DJ	mike (microphone)	rapper	record / LP	turntable

2 *Circle the correct answer.*

1. When did rap music begin?

   a. in the 1960s   **b.** in the 1970s   **c.** in the 1980s   **d.** in the 1990s

2. Where did rap music begin?

   a. in Los Angeles   **b.** in Chicago   **c.** in New York   **d.** in New Orleans

The Rolling Stones

Mozart

Rain (Bi)

Mariah Carey

1 *Find out some information about each famous musician or group. Talk to three different students. Ask each student:*

Do you know anything about _____?

If the student says, "Yes," write the information in your book. If the student says, "No," ask about a different musician on the list. When you finish asking about all the musicians, go on to the next student.

Example

A: Do you know anything about The Rolling Stones?
B: Sure. They're a very famous rock band.
A: OK, thanks. Do you know anything about Mozart?
B: No, I don't. Sorry.

Musician/Group	What I found out
The Rolling Stones	a very famous rock band
Mozart	
Mariah Carey	
Rain (Bi)	

2 *Discuss the questions with the class.*

1. Which famous person or group plays (or played) classical music? Rock? Pop?

2. What did you find out about each musician? (For example, The Rolling Stones is a very famous rock band.)

3. How many people like jazz? Classical music? Rock? Pop music? Rap music? Country?

Jeremy, an American college student, is listening to rap music on a CD. His roommate, Lee, comes into their room.

1 *Read and listen to the conversation.*

LEE:	What kind of music is that?
JEREMY:	It's rap. Do you like it?
LEE:	No, not really. But I don't know much about it.
JEREMY:	Oh, it's so **great**! Do you know how rap started?
LEE:	Uh, no, I have no idea.
JEREMY:	Well, I **just** read a new book about it. **In the 70s**, in New York City, young African Americans started to **play** rap music at parties.
LEE:	At parties? For dancing?
JEREMY:	Yeah. The first rap was dance music.
LEE:	What kinds of instruments did they play?
JEREMY:	They didn't play any **musical instruments**. They used drum machines for the **rhythm**.
LEE:	Oh, and they played old **LPs**[1], right?
JEREMY:	Right. But they played them in a new way.
LEE:	What do you mean?
JEREMY:	Well, some DJs played two songs at the same time. And sometimes they repeated one piece of music again and again.
LEE:	But is it music? Rap doesn't really have a **melody** . . .
JEREMY:	That's true. You don't really "sing" rap. You know, in **slang**, "rap" means "speak."
LEE:	Oh! So "rapping" means "speaking."
JEREMY:	Exactly. **Rappers** wrote songs with words that **rhymed** . . .
LEE:	I know, like "hip a *hop* / And you don't *stop*"!
JEREMY:	Right! And then they *spoke* the words to the **rhythm** of the music.
LEE:	OK, I get it . . .
JEREMY:	And back then, some rappers had big dance parties in the streets.
LEE:	In the streets? Why?
JEREMY:	Because rap started in **poor neighborhoods**. People didn't have money to go to clubs. So they danced to rap music in the streets. And then rap became **popular** all over the country.
LEE:	But rap isn't party music now, is it?
JEREMY:	No way! It changed a lot in the 1980s.

---

[1]**LPs:** long-playing records

2 *How did the first rappers make rap music? Check (✓) all the correct answers.*

The first rappers used _____.

_____ guitars   _____ drum machines   _____ drums

_____ vinyl records (LPs)   _____ African instruments

3 *Write each word or phrase from the box next to its definition.*

great	melody	played	rhymed
in the 70s	musical instruments	poor	rhythm
just	neighborhoods	popular	slang

1. _____ from 1970 to 1979

2. _____ the beat; the tempo; regular sounds in music

3. _____ informal language (i.e., among friends)

4. _____ a short time ago

5. _____ made music (with an instrument, CD, radio, etc.)

6. _____ had the same ending sound (e.g., w<u>alk</u>/t<u>alk</u>)

7. _____ with very little money

8. _____ places in a city where people live

9. _____ very good; excellent

10. _____ a tune; musical notes with a nice sound

11. _____ things you play to make music (e.g., piano, guitar)

12. _____ liked by many people

② FOCUS ON LISTENING

A LISTENING ONE: A Famous Rapper: Tupac Shakur

2 bck

Eli Jones is talking to King Kool. Listen to the beginning of their conversation. Circle the correct answer.

1. Who is Eli Jones?

   a. a rapper   **b.** a radio DJ

2. Why is King Kool on Eli's show?

   a. King Kool wrote a new song about Tupac Shakur.   **b.** King Kool knows a lot about rap music.

3. Eli and King Kool will talk about Tupac Shakur's _____. Check (✓) the words you think are correct.

   ____ childhood   ____ music   ____ problems

   ____ friends   ____ neighborhood   ____ feelings

◀ LISTEN FOR MAIN IDEAS

1 *Read the sentences. Listen to the interview. Write **T** (true) or **F** (false). Correct the false sentences.*

   ____ 1. King Kool was a rapper when he was 70.

   ____ 2. "Rapper's Delight" is a party song.

   ____ 3. The words in rap songs changed in the 1980s.

   ____ 4. In the 80s, rappers wrote songs about the problems in their lives.

   ____ 5. Many rappers were poor.

   ____ 6. Tupac wrote songs because he was in love.

   ____ 7. King Kool thinks Tupac Shakur was the best rapper.

   ____ 8. Young African Americans didn't understand Tupac's songs.

   ____ 9. Tupac's music was popular only when he was alive.

2 *Go back to Section 2A, Question 3. Were your answers correct?*

^{C D 1}
30 *Listen again. Circle the correct answer.*

1. In the 70s, the words in rap songs _____.
   (a.) didn't mean anything   b. didn't rhyme

2. Rappers _____ people to know about the problems in their cities.
   a. wanted   b. didn't want

3. Tupac _____ "gangsta rap."
   (a.) wrote   b. didn't write

4. Tupac *didn't* say, "Guns and drugs are _____."
   a. big problems   (b.) OK to use

5. Tupac Shakur died when he was _____.
   a. 25   b. 35

6. Tupac said, "I'm going to die _____."
   a. rich   b. young

◖ **MAKE INFERENCES**

Listen to the excerpts from Listening One. Circle **two** *correct answers to complete each sentence.*

^{C D 1}
31 **Excerpt One**

1. The DJ thinks that dancing to rap music is _____.
   a. difficult   b. funny   c. popular   d. unusual

^{C D 1}
32 **Excerpt Two**

2. Before Tupac wrote his songs, many people probably _____ about the problems in poor neighborhoods.
   a. knew   b. didn't know   c. cared   d. didn't care

3. King Kool probably thinks the words in his own rap songs _____.
   a. didn't rhyme   b. were not   c. were slang   d. had no
                        important   meaning

^{C D 1}
33 **Excerpt Three**

4. Some people said Tupac's songs were "too real." These people _____ Tupac's songs.
   a. understood   b. didn't   c. liked   d. didn't like
                        understand

 **Excerpt Four**

5. "He wrote about them because **they were in his life**." This sentence has two possible meanings. What are they?

    a. Tupac used guns and drugs.

    b. Tupac didn't use guns or drugs.

    c. Tupac's friends and neighbors used guns and drugs.

    d. Guns and drugs were good things in Tupac's life.

◀ EXPRESS OPINIONS

Discuss the questions in small groups.

1. Do you like songs about real life and problems, or do you like happy dance music? Why?

2. Tupac Shakur died in 1997, but his music is still very popular today. Why do many young people today enjoy Tupac's "old" songs? Will Tupac's music always be popular? Why do you think so?

3. Do you know any other musician who is *not alive* but is still very popular today? Tell about this person and his or her music.

B LISTENING TWO: Rap—Good or Bad?

Listen to the conversation. Match the beginning of each sentence in column A with the end of the sentence in column B.

A	**B**
_____ **1.** Some parents think rap is bad music because it . . .	**a.** must teach their children about right and wrong.
_____ **2.** Mr. Simon thinks that many parents . . .	**b.** tell about rappers' lives.
_____ **3.** Professor Crosby thinks rap is very bad because many teens . . .	**c.** doesn't have a melody or musical instruments.
_____ **4.** Mr. Simon says that rap songs . . .	**d.** copy rappers' bad language and sometimes use guns or drugs.
_____ **5.** Mr. Simon says that parents . . .	**e.** think rap is helpful.
_____ **6.** The principal says that some rap songs . . .	**f.** don't understand rap.
_____ **7.** Some math teachers . . .	**g.** are OK; they're not about using guns.

STEP 1: Organize

What are the positive (good) things about rap music? What are the negative (bad) things? Work with a partner. Complete the sentences in the chart using the information from Listenings One and Two.

POSITIVE	NEGATIVE
1. The songs tell people ... about real things.	**1.** The songs tell people about bad things, such as ... *about tell things such as so*
2. The rhythm is ... *great*	**2.** Rap isn't real music because ... *Play any kind of instrument*
3. People can learn about ...	**3.** The words in rap songs are ... *slang bad words*

STEP 2: Synthesize

King Kool and Professor Crosby meet at WKRZ, the radio station.

Role-play. Work with a new partner. Complete the conversation with information from Step 1: Organize.

KING KOOL: Excuse me, Professor Crosby. My name is King Kool.

PROFESSOR CROSBY: King Kool? Are you a rapper?

KING KOOL: Not now. But I *was* a rapper in the 70s. And I just wrote a book about rap music.

PROFESSOR CROSBY: Teenagers don't need any books about rap music! They know enough about rap.

KING KOOL: Yes, rap is very popular with teens.

PROFESSOR CROSBY: Well, if you ask me, that's not really a good thing.

KING KOOL: Why do you say that?

PROFESSOR CROSBY: ...

KING KOOL: ...

③ FOCUS ON SPEAKING

A VOCABULARY

◖ REVIEW

Work with a partner. Student A, look at this page. Student B, look at Student Activities, pages 208–209. Student A, read line 1. After that, choose the sentence that makes sense. Student B will continue the conversation with you. If you think that your partner chose the wrong sentence, say, "I don't think that makes sense."

Conversation 1: "I don't like rap."

1. Do you like rap music?

   I agree. Rappers are great musicians.
3. OR
   I agree. Rappers are not real musicians.

   That's true. And the words don't even rhyme!
5. OR
   That's true. And the songs are just slang words that rhyme.

   I don't understand it either!
7. OR
   I like it, too.

Switch roles. Now Student B will begin the conversation.

Conversation 2: "Do you like Brazilian jazz?"

   Yeah, I love Brazilian jazz! It has great rhythm.
2. OR
   Yeah, I love rap. It has great rhythm.

   The cool Brazilian singer? Do you have his CD?
4. OR
   The cool Brazilian singer? When did it come out?

   That's old. Where did you buy his new CD?
6. OR
   That's old. Where did you buy it?

   I don't want to buy any CDs. Let's go there now!
8. OR
   I want to buy some jazz CDs. Let's go there now!

1 *Work with a partner. Read the expressions. Then write them on the scale from 0–5.* (**0** *is for very bad feelings, and* **5** *is for very good feelings.*)

It's my favorite (kind of music).	I like it.
I don't like it (at all).	(It's OK, but) I'm not crazy about it.
I love it.	I like it a lot.
I hate it.	I like it very much.
I can take it or leave it.	

5: ____I love it.____   _____

4: _____   _____

3: _____

2: _____   _____

1: _____

0: ____I hate it.____

2 *Share your answers with the class.*

3 *Practice the expressions. Ask two students, "Do you like rap music?" After they answer, ask, "Why do you feel that way?" Then switch roles.*

Work in small groups. Ask and answer the questions. Use the underlined vocabulary and some of the words and phrases in parentheses.

1. Did you ever write a song or a poem? Was it good? Why or why not? (words, rhyme, rhythm, melody)

2. Is there music that you think is bad? If yes, what kind of music is it? Why is it bad? (I hate, I don't like, melody, rhythm, words, etc.)

3. Do you play a musical instrument? If yes, what kind of music do you like to play?

4. Who is a great singer in your country? When was this singer most popular?

5. Do you have a favorite musician? If yes, are this musician's songs about real life?

6. Do you use a lot of slang words when you speak? Why or why not? (I like, I don't like, etc.)

GRAMMAR: Simple Present Tense with Non-Action (Stative) Verbs

1 *Read the sentences. Follow the directions.*

    a. In slang, *rap* means "speak."

    b. They don't play any musical instruments.

    c. I know that rap is very popular.

    d. Young people today still love him.

   1. Underline all the verbs.

   2. Which verbs are non-action verbs? Circle them.

SIMPLE PRESENT TENSE WITH NON-ACTION (STATIVE) VERBS

1. Some verbs are NOT used in the present progressive tense, even when the meaning is "right now."	I **know** that rap is very popular now. *NOT*: ~~I am knowing~~ that rap is very popular.
2. These verbs do NOT describe actions. They describe situations (states), ideas, feelings, and the five senses (see, hear, taste, feel, smell).	I **like** rap music. (That's my *feeling*.) *NOT*: ~~I am liking~~ rap music.
3. Some verbs have two meanings: a non-action meaning and an action meaning.	I **think** you are right. (That's my *idea*.) = non-action meaning BUT: **I'm thinking** about my problem now. (*I'm trying to understand* my problem.) = action meaning
4. Some common verbs with both non-action and action meanings are *feel, have, look, see, smell, taste, think*.	I **have** an iPod®. / **I'm having** a party. (*I own*) = (*I'm organizing*) = non-action meaning action meaning

2 Work with a partner. Look at the sentences. Some verbs are action verbs and some verbs are "non-action" (stative) verbs. Decide what each verb tells about. Write the verb in the correct column in the chart.

1. In slang, rap **means** "speak."
2. They don't **play** any musical instruments.
3. I **know** that rap **is** very popular.
4. Young people today still **love** him.
5. A lot of people don't **understand** Tupac.
6. I **like** it a lot.
7. I **want** to tell you about a big problem.
8. And then what **happens**?
9. I **believe** that it **is** very bad for our children!
10. But our children **hear** this music every day.
11. The children **think** rappers are cool.
12. The songs **have** no melody.
13. They don't **sing**.
14. They **listen** to it on their iPods.

NON-ACTION (STATIVE) VERBS				ACTION VERBS
Situation	Idea	Feeling	Sense	
means	know			play
is				

3 Read the conversation silently. Circle the correct form of the verb in parentheses—simple present or present progressive. Remember, if the verb is not about an action (stative), don't use **-ing**. Then read the conversation aloud with a partner.

Brian and Dennis are sitting on a bus. Brian is listening to his iPod.

DENNIS: Brian, take off your headphones for a minute! You (**1.** *listen /* ~~are listening~~) to Tupac Shakur, right?

BRIAN: Yes, (**2.** *I do / I am*), but how (**3.** *do you know / are you knowing*) that?

DENNIS: Because the music (**4.** *is / is being*) too loud! I (**5.** *hear / am hearing*) the song you (**6.** *listen / are listening*) to. And I (**7.** *know / am knowing*) Tupac Shakur's voice.

BRIAN: Oh, sorry.

DENNIS: (**8.** *Do you see / Are you seeing*) those women over there? (**9.** *They look / They're looking*) at you! I (**10.** *think / am thinking*) they're really angry.

BRIAN: OK, OK, I (**11.** *turn / am turning*) the volume[1] down. With rap music, I (**12.** *need / am needing*) to raise the volume. If the volume (**13.** *is / is being*) too low, I (**14.** *don't hear / am not hearing*) all the words, and then I (**15.** *don't really understand / am not really understanding*) the song.

DENNIS: Yeah, I (**16.** *know / am knowing*) what you (**17.** *mean / are meaning*).

BRIAN: And in Tupac's songs, the words are so important. I (**18.** *want / am wanting*) to hear everything.

DENNIS: I (**19.** *understand / am understanding*). But everyone on this bus (**20.** *hates / is hating*) you now! Let's get off here and walk.

BRIAN: Good idea!

---

[1]**volume:** the amount of sound that something makes

◀ PRONUNCIATION: /ɪ/ vs. /iy/

PRONOUNCING /ɪ/ AND /iy/

/ɪ/ is the vowel sound in the word *it* /ɪt/.
Relax your lips (don't smile).
Make your tongue a LITTLE BIT lower than for /iy/.
Pull your tongue back a LITTLE BIT more than for /iy/.

/iy/ is the vowel sound in the word *eat* /iyt/.
Spread your lips very wide, like a smile.
The front of your tongue is high in your mouth.

1 *Listen to the words and repeat them.*

/ɪ/	/iy/
1. think	10. believe
2. opinion	11. repeat
3. musician	12. piece
4. rhythm	13. agree
5. instruments	14. people
6. sing	15. teens
7. listen	16. beat
8. hip-hop	17. mean
9. big	18. machine

2 ᶜᴰ⁷ ⟨37⟩ *Listen to the words and repeat them. Then listen again and circle the word you hear.*

1. **a.** bit   2. **a.** live   3. **a.** it   4. **a.** ship   5. **a.** sit

     b. beat   **b.** leave   **b.** eat   **b.** sheep   **b.** seat

3 *Take turns with a partner. Choose a word from Exercise 2. Ask your partner how to spell the word. Pronounce the vowel clearly so your partner knows which word to spell. If your partner spells the wrong word, say your word again. Do this with four words.*

Example

A: How do you spell _____live_____?
B: L-I-V-E.
A: That's right.

4 ᶜᴰ⁷ ⟨38⟩ *Listen to the conversation and repeat it. Then practice the conversation in groups of three.*

Ian and Bill are roommates. They live in Apartment 3C. Pete lives upstairs in Apartment 4C. It's two o'clock in the morning.

IAN: I can't sleep.
BILL: I can't sleep either.
IAN: I think the people in 4C are having a party.
BILL: But I need to sleep!
IAN: Me too. Let's go talk to them.

Ian and Bill go upstairs. They ring the bell and knock on Pete's door, but no one comes.

BILL: I don't think they can hear us.
IAN: Of course not. The music is too loud.

Ian and Bill both knock together. The door opens.

IAN: Hi. We live in 3C.
BILL: Yeah. And we can't sleep. The music, you know?
PETE: Oh yeah. I'm really sorry. Umm, do you want to come in?

IAN and **BILL** (looking at each other): Well, uh, I don't know . . . OK.

PETE: The party's almost over[1]. But there's still a little food, and you can meet my friends.

---

[1]**over:** finished

When we say our opinion, we usually begin with a phrase such as "I think."

Here are some other useful phrases you can use:

I believe . . .	I think . . .	In my opinion, . . .
I feel . . .	If you ask me, . . .	

I think Tupac Shakur was the greatest rapper ever.

In my opinion, rappers are very bad examples for young people.

If you ask me, they aren't real musicians.

I believe that rap is very bad for our children.

1 *Work in groups of three or four. One student reads the introduction aloud.*

Introduction: Using Rap Music in School

> Many children don't like school. Some teachers think that when they teach with rap songs, children like school more and learn more. Other teachers don't agree. They say that rap doesn't help students learn.

2 *Now take turns. Choose one statement from the next page. Read it aloud and tell your opinion about it. Remember to use the phrases for expressing opinions.*

Example

Statement: A kindergarten teacher says, "In my class, children learn the ABCs and easy math (1 + 1 = 2, 2 + 2 = 4, etc.) in a rap song. The rhythm and rhyme help them remember."

OPINION: **If you ask me,** that's a great idea! **I think** it's fun to learn with songs. **I believe** children can learn very easy things, like the ABCs, in a song. But **I don't think** children can learn everything in rap songs.

Statements

1. Elementary school students learn a rap song by the famous rapper, Nas. The name of the song is "I Can." The song says that drugs are bad for young people. It tells them to stay in school and study hard.

2. A middle-school teacher says, "The young students in my class can learn all the words to a hip-hop song in one day. So, I think teachers can write rap songs about math or history, and the students can learn them quickly, too."

3. One professor studied music and learning. He says, "Some kinds of music help people learn. For example, classical music helps people learn math. But rap music does not help people learn. Maybe they will remember new things for a short time, but not for a long time."

4. One high school English teacher says, "My students are interested in TV, DVDs, music, and video games. They are not interested in school. So, I teach them about something they like." The students in his class read rap songs, discuss them, and write essays about them.

5. One college professor says, "When students take tests, the tests will *not* be in rap. These students will not know how to pass their tests. Teaching with rap music is a very bad idea."

◀ **PRODUCTION: Student Interviews**

> *In this activity, you are going to interview your classmates. Find out what kinds of music they like and dislike.* Then share the information with the class. Try to use the vocabulary, grammar, pronunciation, and language for expressing likes and dislikes and opinions from the unit.*

Follow the steps.

Step 1: Think of four kinds of music—two kinds that you *like*, and two kinds that you *don't like* (e.g., like: reggae and classical music, don't like: jazz and rock).

Step 2: On a piece of paper, write one kind of music in each corner. Write ONLY the name of the music.

---

*For Alternative Speaking Topics, see page 63.

Step 3: Hold the paper in front of you. Walk around the room and talk to six classmates, one by one. Look at the students' papers. What kinds of music *do* they like? What kinds of music *don't* they like? Ask questions about the music on their paper.

Example

A: Hi, can I ask you a question?
B: OK. / Why not? / Sure.
A: Do you like classical music?

IF YOU LIKE IT	IF YOU DON'T LIKE IT
<u>Student B</u>: Yes (Yeah), **I like it a lot.**	<u>Student B</u>: (It's OK, but) **I'm not crazy about it.**
<u>Student A</u>: Why do you like it?	<u>Student A</u>: Why do you feel that way?
<u>Student B</u>: **In my opinion**, it's the most beautiful music in the world. **I like it** because . . . (tell your reason). **I think** the melodies are beautiful. I understand the feelings in the music. your answer: _____	<u>Student B</u>: Well, **if you ask me,** it's boring. **I don't like it** because . . . (tell your reason). I don't understand it. **I feel** it's too slow. your answer: _____

A: Oh, OK. / OK, thanks. / Oh, that's interesting. Thanks.

Step 4: Share some of your information with the class.

ALTERNATIVE SPEAKING TOPICS

Discuss one of the topics. Use the vocabulary and grammar from the unit.

1. In some places, CDs have labels[1] on them. The labels tell if the CDs' songs have bad language or are about guns or sex. If you want to buy these CDs, you must be 17 years old or older. Many parents are happy about this. Their children cannot buy "bad" songs. Many teenagers are angry about this. They like rap and gangsta rap. They want to buy these CDs.

   What's your opinion? Is it a good idea to sell these CDs *only* to teenagers over 17? Why or why not?

   Use the language for Expressing Opinions in your answer (**If you ask me**, **I feel**, **I believe**, etc.).

2. Rap is not new music anymore. What kind of music is new today? Tell about a new kind of music. It could be from your country or from any other country you know about. Tell who started this kind of music and who plays it now. Is the musician or group famous? Is the music popular? Who listens to it?

RESEARCH TOPICS, see page 215.

RESEARCH TOPICS, see page 215.

---

[1]**labels:** small pieces of paper with writing

History

No   No   N

MR   netshes
     ne-shes

No   No   Nc

Something Valuable

1. _____

2. _____

3. _____   4.

①FOCUS ON THE TOPIC

A PREDICT

Look at the picture. Discuss the question with the class.

What jewelry do you see? Write each word on the line next to the object it describes.

4	2	1	3
bracelet	earrings	necklace	ring

Work in groups of three. Write the names of the students in your group. Discuss the questions in the chart. Write each student's answers. Then report one interesting answer to the class.

	STUDENT 1 (YOU)	STUDENT 2	STUDENT 3
1. Do you wear jewelry?	No	No	No
2. What kind of jewelry do you like? Rings? Necklaces? Bracelets? Earrings?	MR	Neklaes necklaces	
3. Is jewelry popular in your country?	No	No	No
4. In your country, do both men and women wear jewelry?	No	No	No
5. What kind of jewelry do women wear? What do men wear?			
6. In your country, do women or men get diamond[1] jewelry before they get married?			

―――――――――――
[1]**diamond:** a clear, hard jewel

Read and listen to the passage about great moments in diamond history. Then, write each boldfaced word next to its definition on the next page.

Great Moments in Diamond History

Many people are interested in the **history** of diamonds. Here are some important moments in diamond history.

1200s:	English kings and queens begin to collect the **valuable** Crown Jewels.
1500s:	The king of France buys jewels from India. They **are worth** a lot of money.
1600s:	**Wealthy** women in Europe get diamond engagement rings.
1800s:	People find diamonds in South Africa. Some are small, but others are **huge**. These diamonds **weigh more** than the small ones.
late 1800s:	Cecil Rhodes starts the De Beers Group in South Africa. It soon controls 90 percent of the diamonds in the world. Workers for De Beers have to live in special areas. Their bosses watch them. The bosses don't want them to **steal** diamonds.
1940s:	Advertisements for De Beers diamonds **appear** in American magazines. More Americans buy diamond engagement rings.
1980s:	De Beers **advertises** in Japan. De Beers tells the Japanese, "a diamond is forever."
2006:	Diamond engagement rings are a part of many Japanese weddings. In these weddings, people still follow Japanese **traditions**. For example, they drink sake (rice wine) for good **luck**.

steal **a.** take something that doesn't belong to you

neighbor **b.** rich

appear **c.** are seen by people

valuable **d.** expensive

Advertises **e.** uses words or photographs to tell people to buy something

worth **f.** are heavier

tradition **g.** beliefs or customs from one culture

huge **h.** very big

luck **i.** good or bad things that happen by chance

history **j.** things that happened in the past

are worth **k.** cost

②FOCUS ON LISTENING

A **LISTENING ONE: The Hope Diamond**

The Hope Diamond

CD 1 40 *Listen to the beginning of "The Hope Diamond." Read the sentences. Check (✓) Yes, No, or I Don't Know.*

	Yes	No	I Don't Know
1. The people are in a museum.	✓	○	○
2. The Hope Diamond is valuable.	✓	○	○
3. The Hope Diamond is new.	○	✓	○

1 ᶜᴰ⁷ **41** *Read the sentences. Listen to "The Hope Diamond." Put the sentences in order from 1 to 3.*

____1____ King Louis XIV (the fourteenth) of France buys the Hope Diamond.

____3____ A wealthy woman buys the diamond and has bad luck.

____2____ Henry Philip Hope buys the Hope Diamond.

2 *Go back to Section 2A on page 68. Were your answers correct?*

◖ LISTEN FOR DETAILS

ᶜᴰ⁷ **42** *Listen again. Circle the correct answer to complete each sentence.*

1. The Hope Diamond is the most valuable diamond in ____.
   a. London
   b. the world

2. The Hope Diamond comes from ____.
   a. France
   b. India

3. The Hope Diamond moves to different places, and it gets ____.
   a. smaller
   b. prettier

4. No one can find the Hope Diamond in 1792 because somebody ____.
   a. loses it
   b. steals it

5. The name of this diamond ____.
   a. is a man's family name
   b. means a wish for good luck

6. The woman who buys the Hope Diamond loses ____.
   a. her family
   b. her money

◀ **MAKE INFERENCES**

Listen to the excerpts from Listening One. Circle the answers. Then discuss your answers with the class.

C D 7
43 **Excerpt One**

1. Bob _____ the story of the Hope Diamond.
   a. knows
   b. thinks he knows

C D 7
44 **Excerpt Two**

2. Katelyn _____ the meaning of "Hope" in the name "Hope Diamond."
   a. knows
   b. doesn't know

C D 7
45 **Excerpt Three**

3. Bob _____ the Hope Diamond was bad luck.
   a. believes
   b. doesn't believe

◀ **EXPRESS OPINIONS**

Do you agree or disagree with the statements? Circle your answer. Then discuss your answers in a small group. Explain your opinions.

1. A diamond can bring you happiness.	Agree	Disagree
2. A diamond can bring you bad luck.	Agree	Disagree
3. You need a diamond to get married.	Agree	Disagree

B **LISTENING TWO: The Four Cs**

C D 7
1 **46** *Listen to the radio advertisement.*

2 *Complete each sentence with* **cut, color, clarity,** *or* **carat.**

1. Good diamonds usually do not have any __color__.

2. __cut__ makes a diamond sparkle[1].

3. __carat__ is how much a diamond weighs.

4. Good diamonds are very clear; they have __clarity__.

_____
[1]**sparkle:** shine

◀ STEP 1: Organize

*Work in a small group. Read the questions in the chart. Check (✓) the answers.
There may be more than one correct answer. Use information from Listenings
One and Two. Give reasons for your answers.*

	CUT	COLOR	CLARITY	CARAT
1. Why did King Louis XIV of France want to buy the Hope Diamond?				
2. Why is the Hope Diamond so valuable today?				
3. What does an excellent diamond have?				
4. What don't most valuable diamonds have?				

◀ STEP 2: Synthesize

A salesperson is helping a shopper buy a pair of diamond earrings.

*Role-play. Work with a partner. Complete the conversation with information from
Step 1: Organize.*

SALESPERSON: Can I help you?
SHOPPER: Yes. I'd like to buy a pair of diamond earrings.
SALESPERSON: Here are some beautiful one-carat earrings.
SHOPPER: No thanks. They're too . . .
SALESPERSON: Here's a half-carat pair. Look how they sparkle.
SHOPPER: I see. They have a very nice . . .
SALESPERSON: . . .
SHOPPER: . . .

A VOCABULARY

REVIEW

Work with a partner. Complete the conversation with words from the box. Read the conversation aloud together. Then switch roles and read it again.

carats	history	sparkles	valuable	worth
fascinating	huge	steals	wealthy	

TOUR GUIDE: The Hope Diamond is _____ a lot of money.
1.

TOURIST: Yes, I know it's very _____.
2.

TOUR GUIDE: As you can see, it's also very large.

TOURIST: Wow! It's _____. How many carats is the diamond?
3.

TOUR GUIDE: It is more than 40 _____.
4.

TOURIST: This diamond is beautiful.

TOUR GUIDE: Yes, it's beautiful because it _____. Are you
5.

interested in _____?
6.

TOURIST: Yes, I think learning about the past is _____.
7.

TOUR GUIDE: Well, listen to the diamond's story. In 1792, someone

_____ the diamond from its owner in France.
8.

TOURIST: Then the diamond appears in London in 1812, right?

TOUR GUIDE: Right. After that, a _____ man buys the diamond.
9.

TOURIST: What was his name?

TOUR GUIDE: Henry Philip Hope.

TOURIST: Oh, so *that's* how the diamond got its name!

🔵 *Read and listen to the review of the movie **Blood Diamond** (2006). Match*
47 *the boldfaced words and phrases to their definitions.*

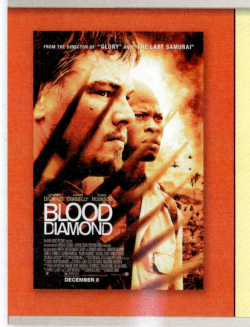

Blood Diamond is the story of a poor diamond worker in Sierra Leone, a country in West Africa. He finds a huge diamond. This is a very **lucky find**. It is very hard to find a diamond like this. The diamond is worth **a fortune**. The diamond worker wants to **do the right thing**— he wants to use the diamond to help his family. But some **selfish** people try to take the diamond away from the diamond worker. They don't care about him. They care only about themselves. They say that it is just **tough luck** for him. They are **heartless**. However, a man named Danny helps the diamond worker and his family. Leonardo DiCaprio plays this role. DiCaprio is an excellent actor in *Blood Diamond*.

_____ **1.** lucky find	**a.** thinking only about themselves
_____ **2.** do the right thing	**b.** a lot of money
_____ **3.** a fortune	**c.** not caring about other people
_____ **4.** tough luck	**d.** valuable discovery
_____ **5.** selfish	**e.** act in the correct way
_____ **6.** heartless	**f.** bad luck

◖ CREATE

Work in small groups. Take turns asking and answering the questions. Use the underlined words in your conversation.

1. Some diamonds are worth <u>a fortune</u>. What are some other things that are worth <u>a fortune</u>?

2. Tell about a time when you <u>did the right thing</u>. What did you do?

(continued on next page)

3. What is an example of <u>selfish</u> behavior?

4. Losing a valuable possession[1] is one kind of <u>tough luck</u>. Did you ever have <u>tough luck</u>? What happened?

B GRAMMAR: The Simple Present

1 *Read the sentences. Then answer the questions.*

    a. That diamond really sparkles.

    b. A valuable diamond weighs a lot.

    c. We want to look at some rings.

    d. The name doesn't mean "hope" or "bad luck."

    e. Small diamonds don't cost as much as large diamonds.

    f. You need a lot of money to buy a diamond.

    g. Do you have any rings?

1. Which verbs end in *-s*?

2. Which sentences are negative? What are the verbs in these sentences?

3. Which sentence is a *yes / no* question?

THE SIMPLE PRESENT	
1. Use the simple present tense for everyday actions or facts.	Millions of people **visit** the museum every year. The diamond **weighs** a lot.
2. When the subject is *he*, *she*, or *it*, put an *s* at the end of the main verb. **NOTE:** *Be* and *have* are irregular.	She **likes** jewelry. It **costs** a lot of money. BE: *am*, *is*, *are* (See Unit 1.) It **is** a valuable diamond. HAVE: This diamond **has** a fascinating history. My sisters **have** diamond rings.
3. To form negative statements with contractions, use ***doesn't* or *don't* + the base form of the verb**	He **doesn't like** diamonds. You **don't have** a ring.

---

[1]**possession:** something you own

4. For **yes / no** questions, use **Do (or Does)** + subject + the base form of the verb	**Do you see** the ring? **Does it sparkle?**
5. For **wh-** questions, use **Wh-** word + **do (or does)** + subject + the base form of the verb	**What do you want** to buy? **Where do you like** to go shopping? **How much does that ring cost?**

2 *Bob and Katelyn are in London on their honeymoon. They are visiting the Tower of London. Complete the sentences with the present tense of the verbs.*

TOUR GUIDE: Welcome to the Tower of London and to the Crown Jewels! Are the Crown Jewels real? How much are they worth? Visitors always _____*ask*_____ these two questions. The answer to
      1. (ask)
the first question is easy: Of course the jewels are real! And they are old. You _____ them in old paintings and
                              2. (see)
_____ about them in history books. But we
   3. (read)
_____ the answer to the second question. These
   4. (not know)
jewels are worth more than gold and diamonds. They are an important part of 800 years of English history.

We still _____ the crowns. When a person
            5. (use)
_____ king or queen, he or she
   6. (become)

The Crown Jewels

_____ one of the crowns. And when Parliament[1]
7. (wear)

_____ every year, the Queen _____
8. (open)   **9. (wear)**

the crown. _____ you _____ the
10. (see)

huge and sparkling Koh-i-Noor Diamond? It

_____ 106 carats. The name means "mountain of
11. (weigh)

light." It _____ like a mountain of light! It
12. (sparkle)

_____ from India and it belonged to Queen
13. (come)

Victoria. People think that this diamond _____
14. (bring)

bad luck to all men, so only women _____ it!
15. (wear)

BOB: Katelyn, _____ you _____ it? It
16. (believe)

_____ like the same story again! The Hope
17. (sound)

Diamond _____ bad luck, too.
18. (bring)

KATELYN: I know. Huge diamonds _____ huge stories!
19. (have)

C   SPEAKING

◖ PRONUNCIATION: -S Endings for Present Tense

1 CD 7 *Listen to the underlined verbs in the conversation. The present tense ending*
🔘 *-s has three different pronunciations.*

A: Your mother has a huge diamond!
B: She <u>loves</u> that ring. It was her mother's. She only <u>takes</u> it off to clean it.
A: Clean it? How do you clean a diamond?
B: With toothpaste! She <u>brushes</u> her ring with toothpaste.

Look at the three underlined verbs in the conversation. Answer this question
for each verb: Does the *-s* ending add a new syllable or just a new sound?

In the present tense, the pronunciation of the third-person singular ending
depends on the last sound of the *base form* of the verb.

_____
[1]**Parliament:** the building of the British government

PRONOUNCING -S ENDINGS FOR PRESENT TENSE

1. Pronounce the **-s ending /əz/ or /ɪz/ after /s, z, ʃ, ʒ, tʃ, dʒ/.** (See the phonetic alphabet on page 238.) After these sounds, the -s ending adds a new syllable.	use (one syllable) ⟶ uses (two syllables) She **uses** toothpaste to clean her ring. Tom **washes** the jewelry store windows every day. The salesperson **watches** the jewelry carefully.
2. Pronounce the **-s ending /s/ after /p, t, k, f/.** The -s ending is a final sound.	She **keeps** her jewelry in a special box. He **wants** to keep the huge diamond. The ring **looks** beautiful.
3. Pronounce the **-s ending /z/ after all other sounds.** The -s ending is a final sound.	She never **wears** jewelry. The jewelry store **stays** open late. The store manager **arrives** at 8:00 A.M.

2 ᶜᴰ🔹 *Listen to the conversation and repeat the lines. Then practice the*
conversation with a partner.

A: My roommate <u>wants</u> to see *Blood Diamond* tonight. Do you want to see it with us?

B: Sure. What time? My class <u>ends</u> at 7:30, but the professor never <u>finishes</u> on time. Sometimes she <u>teaches</u> until almost 8:00 P.M.!

A: No problem. We're going to watch it on a DVD at my house. Just come whenever she <u>lets</u> you out.

B: Is it a long movie?

A: I don't know. It probably <u>lasts</u> a couple of hours.

B: OK. I'll see you around eight o'clock, I hope. I'll bring the popcorn.

3 *Circle the pronunciation of the* **-s** *ending of the underlined words. Then check your answers with a classmate's and take turns reading the sentences.*

1. Sonia <u>wears</u> her ring all the time. It <u>looks</u> expensive.

əz / s / (z)   əz / s / z

2. Alex <u>buys</u> and <u>sells</u> diamonds to celebrities. He <u>travels</u> all over the world.

əz / s / z   əz / s / z   əz / s / z

3. My roommate really <u>likes</u> jewelry. She <u>buys</u> something new every week.

əz / s / z   əz / s / z

   She <u>uses</u> all her money to buy jewelry!

əz / s / z

(continued on next page)

4. The movie <u>starts</u> at 9:00. It <u>takes</u> about an hour to get there, so let's leave
əz / s / z   əz / s / z

before 8:00.

5. The jewelry store <u>opens</u> at 9 A.M. and <u>closes</u> at 6:00 P.M.
əz / s / z   əz / s / z

4 *Work with a partner to complete your schedule. Student A, look at your schedule at the bottom of this page. Student B, look at Student Activities page 210. Use the model to ask your partner for the missing information. Use the verbs in your chart to tell Student B the information she / he is missing. Do the example:*

Example

A: Do you know about <u>the bus from New York to Kingston?</u>

B: Yes, <u>it leaves at 2 P.M. and arrives at 3:45.</u>

STUDENT A'S SCHEDULE	TIMES	
The bus from New York to Kingston	_____	_____

STUDENT B'S SCHEDULE	TIMES	
The bus from New York to Kingston (leave, arrive)	2 P.M.	3:45 P.M.

STUDENT A'S SCHEDULE	TIMES	
The Hope Diamond tour (verbs: begin, end)	4 P.M.	5:15 P.M.
The museum (verbs: open, close)	10 A.M.	7 P.M.
The movie *Blood Diamond*	_____	_____
The train from New York to Montreal, Canada	_____	_____

"Will you marry me?" is a marriage proposal. It is a special kind of suggestion. Other suggestions are about something we want to do or think someone else should do. They can begin with "Why don't we ...?," "Let's ...," or "How about ...?"

Why don't we (+ base verb) ...?	**BOB:** *Why don't we go in and look at rings?*
Let's (+ base verb) ...	**KATELYN:** OK. *Let's look at the diamonds.*
How about (+ -ing verb) ...?	**BOB:** *How about starting with that one?* **KATELYN:** Good idea.

1 *Read the conversation. Write suggestions using the words in parentheses. Use the correct form of the verbs. Then practice the conversation with a partner. Take turns reading A and B.*

1. **A:** I want to buy my mother a pearl necklace.

   B: _____ (go to a jewelry store downtown)

2. **A:** Good idea. There are a lot of jewelry shops downtown. But I can't drive today. My car isn't working.

   B: _____ (take the bus)

3. **A:** OK. Can you go right now?

   B: _____ (no, tomorrow)

   A: OK. That's fine with me.

2 *Complete the conversation. Use all three ways to make suggestions. Then practice the conversation aloud with a partner.*

A: _____ to the movies later?

B: OK. _____ to the Ritz Theater.

A: The Ritz is so far away. _____ to the Central Theater?

B: OK. Good idea.

3 *Work with a partner. Make up a short conversation like the one in Exercise 2. Then role-play it for the class.*

> **In this activity, you will role-play a conversation.** Work in groups of four. You are friends. You are walking down the street together. One of you finds a diamond bracelet. It looks very valuable. Have a conversation about what to do with the bracelet. Try to use the vocabulary, grammar, pronunciation, and language for making suggestions from the unit.*

Follow the steps.

Step 1: Divide your group into two pairs, A and B.

Pair A: You don't want to keep the bracelet. You want to find the owner. You want to do the right thing.

Pair B: You want to take the bracelet. You really need money right now. You want to sell the bracelet for cash.

Step 2: With your partner, prepare some sentences that you can say to the other pair.

Step 3: Have a conversation between Pair A and Pair B. In your conversation, you disagree with each other about what to do with the bracelet. Finally, you all make one decision.

Example

(Students 1 and 2 are from Pair A. Students 3 and 4 are from Pair B.)

Student 1: We can't keep this bracelet.
Student 3: I want to keep it. I think it's valuable.
Student 2: You're selfish. We need to find the owner.
Student 4: Why don't we try to sell it? We all need money . . .

Step 4: Practice your conversation. Make sure that you have a clear decision at the end. Then tell the class what your group decided and why.

---

*For Alternative Speaking Topics, see page 81.

ALTERNATIVE SPEAKING TOPICS

Discuss one of the topics. Use the vocabulary and grammar from the unit.

1. Tell the story of a piece of jewelry or other valuable possession in your family. How did your family get it? Who keeps it now? Who will get it in the future?

2. What makes a piece of jewelry valuable? Is it the cost, the sentimental value[1], or something else?

3. Do you think that jewelry is a good gift? Why or why not?

RESEARCH TOPICS, see page 217.

———
[1] **sentimental value:** a value you give something because it comes from a person you love

Together Is Better

① FOCUS ON THE TOPIC

A PREDICT

Discuss the questions with the class.

1. Look at the title. What does it mean?
2. Look at the photo. Who are the people? What are they doing?

1 *Look at the cartoon. Why is it funny? Share your ideas with a partner.*

2 *Look at the cartoon for one minute. Then close your book and draw everything you can remember from the cartoon.*

3 *Compare your picture with a partner's. Then look at the cartoon again and discuss the questions.*

1. Which things did you forget?

2. Who remembered more things?

3. Did you remember any of the same things? Any different things?

4 *Discuss the questions with the class.*

1. What do you usually remember? (people's names, birthdays, etc.)

2. What do you often forget?

3. Do you agree or disagree with this statement? *Older people often forget things.*

4. Do you know anyone who has (or had) Alzheimer's disease? Tell a few things about this person.

1 🔊 *Read and listen to the radio advertisement.*

RHODA S.:   *"I can't enjoy a book or a movie anymore because when I get to the middle, I can't remember the beginning."* (a 67-year-old woman with Alzheimer's disease)

JAMES M.:   *"Sometimes I'm going someplace. Then I don't remember where I'm going."* (a 74-year-old man with Alzheimer's disease)

Does someone you love say things like this? He or she may have Alzheimer's **disease**. Please listen . . . We can help. Twenty-six million people in the world have Alzheimer's disease. People with Alzheimer's disease can't remember things. First, they **forget** what they're doing. Then they forget how to drive a car or cook. They often **get lost**, even in their own neighborhood. Then they **lose** their **memories**. They forget what they did yesterday or last week. Later they don't remember their friends and **relatives**. Many people with Alzheimer's lose their friends. They feel **lonely**, like Sarah, a 68-year-old woman. Sarah told us, "My friends don't visit me anymore. When people know you have Alzheimer's, you never see them again."

Doctors have no cure[1] for Alzheimer's, but at the Alzheimer's Organization, our psychologists are trying to help. We have support[2] groups. Anyone with Alzheimer's disease can **join** our support groups. The support group **members get together** with a psychologist. They talk with the psychologist and with each other. They help each other. They make new friends in the group. Then they don't feel so lonely anymore. So, if you have a friend or a relative with Alzheimer's disease, please call us today. We can help.

2 *Circle the correct answer.*

At the Alzheimer's Organization, people with Alzheimer's _____.

a. meet a special group of psychologists.

b. meet together in a special group.

---

[1]**cure:** a drug or medicine that brings health

[2]**support:** help

3 *Work with a partner. Take turns. Student A, read the sentence with the underlined vocabulary. Ask the question about the meaning. Student B, choose the correct meaning and answer the question.*

Example

A: Twenty-six million people have Alzheimer's <u>disease</u>. What does *disease* mean?
(**a.** medicine or cure;   **b.** sickness or illness)

B: *Disease* means <u>sickness or illness</u>.

1. People with Alzheimer's often <u>forget</u> what they're doing. What does *forget* mean?
(**a.** give away;   **b.** don't remember)

2. People with Alzheimer's sometimes <u>get lost</u>. They don't know how to find their home. What does *get lost* mean?
(**a.** don't know where they are;   **b.** can't find their house key)

3. People with Alzheimer's sometimes <u>lose</u> their friends. What does *lose* mean?
(**a.** keep;   **b.** can't keep)

4. People with Alzheimer's always lose their <u>memories</u>. What are *memories*?
(**a.** things that people remember about the past;   **b.** things that people do)

5. Many people with Alzheimer's disease feel <u>lonely</u>, like Sarah. What does *lonely* mean?
(**a.** sad because they don't have friends;   **b.** afraid because they are alone)

6. People with Alzheimer's can <u>join</u> our support groups. What does *join* mean?
(**a.** be a leader of a group;   **b.** be a member of a group)

7. The group <u>members</u> get together to talk and help each other. Who are *members*?
(**a.** people in a group;   **b.** people who remember many things)

8. The group members <u>get together</u> to talk and help each other. What does *get together* mean?
(**a.** meet;   **b.** have a party)

9. People with Alzheimer's often forget their <u>relatives</u>—their husbands, wives, and children. Who are *relatives*?
(**a.** people in their family;   **b.** good friends)

2 FOCUS ON LISTENING

A LISTENING ONE: I Remember

Dr. Alan Dienstag with a support group

Jane Oliver works at the Alzheimer's Organization. Every month, the families of people with Alzheimer's disease have a meeting there. They want to learn how to help their relatives.

*CD7 Jane Oliver is introducing Dr. Alan Dienstag. Dr. Dienstag works with people who have Alzheimer's. Do you think Dr. Dienstag will talk about the things below? Listen. Then check (✓) **Yes** or **No**.*

	Yes	No			Yes	No
1. New medicines	○	○	**5.** Bad memories		○	○
2. Listening to music	○	○	**6.** Childhood memories		○	○
3. Writing stories	○	○	**7.** Remembering names		○	○
4. Making friends	○	○	**8.** Joining support groups		○	○

◖ LISTEN FOR MAIN IDEAS

1 *CD7 Listen to the conversation. Write **T** (true) or **F** (false). Correct the false information.*

_____ **1.** The support group is a writers' group.

_____ **2.** The group members write about Alzheimer's disease.

(continued on next page)

_____ **3.** The members discuss each other's stories.

_____ **4.** People with Alzheimer's usually remember the past.

_____ **5.** The members help each other to remember words.

_____ **6.** The members discuss how they feel.

_____ **7.** Sometimes the members are happy to get together.

2 *Go back to Section 2A on page 87. Were your answers correct?*

◖ LISTEN FOR DETAILS

CD 1
(53) *Listen again. Circle the correct answer.*

1. Who started the writers' group?
   a. Jane Oliver
   b. Dr. Dienstag
   c. a medical doctor

2. How often does the writers' group meet?
   a. once a week
   b. twice a week
   c. every month

3. How do the group members feel after they write a story?
   a. They feel tired.
   b. They feel good.
   c. They feel surprised.

4. Why do the group members become good friends?
   a. They are all good writers.
   b. They have the same psychologist.
   c. They understand each other's feelings.

5. What are the first words of every story?
   a. "I don't remember."
   b. "I'm a member."
   c. "I remember."

6. Why are the group members happy to get together?
   a. They need to finish their stories.
   b. They have a good time together.
   c. They all have a terrible disease.

Listen to the excerpts from Listening One. Circle the correct answer to complete each sentence.

⟨54⟩ Excerpt One

1. Many people probably think that a writers' group for people with Alzheimer's is ____.
   a. a strange idea
   b. a great idea

⟨55⟩ Excerpt Two

2. The speaker doesn't think that ____.
   a. her father has Alzheimer's disease
   b. writing a story can help her father

⟨56⟩ Excerpt Three

3. Dr. Dienstag thinks the group members feel good because they ____.
   a. remembered a lot from their past
   b. did something difficult

⟨57⟩ Excerpt Four

4. The woman probably thinks that people with Alzheimer's ____.
   a. feel lonely
   b. have nice friends

◀ **EXPRESS OPINIONS**

Discuss the questions in small groups.

1. How can writing stories help people with different diseases?

2. What other support groups do you know about? How do they help?

CD 7
58
Listen to Elsa, a member of the writers' group. She is reading her story to Dr. Dienstag and the other members of the group. Complete each sentence with a word from the box.

clouds	fish	name
finished	memory	words

1. Elsa's story is about a childhood _____.

2. The _____ in the sky looked like the waves in the sea.

3. Elsa forgot the special _____ of that kind of sky.

4. Elsa wanted to remember the name of a _____.

5. A group member helped Elsa to find the right _____ for her story.

6. Elsa's story is not _____.

Mackerel fish

Mackerel sky

INTEGRATE LISTENINGS ONE AND TWO

◀ **STEP 1: Organize**

1 *Think about Dr. Dienstag's group and Elsa's story.*

    a. *Think about all the things that people with Alzheimer's disease can't remember and can't do anymore. What did they "lose"?*

    b. *Then think about the members of the Alzheimer's writers' group. What did they "find"?*

2 *Work with a partner to complete the two lists. Choose from the phrases in the box. (You will not use all of the phrases.)*

~~their memories~~	their independence[1]
a cure for Alzheimer's disease	something they can do well
~~new friends~~	a new job
their cars	their jobs
their old life	a place to talk about their feelings
a new hobby	their old friends
their relatives	people who understand them

People *with* Alzheimer's Disease Lost:

    their memories

_____

_____

_____

_____

People *in the* Writers' Group Found:

    new friends

_____

_____

_____

3 *Now compare your lists with your classmates'.*

---

[1]**independence:** the ability to live by yourself, without help

Sarah is a 68-year old woman with Alzheimer's disease. Her daughter, Jennifer, tells her about the writers' group. Jennifer thinks it's a great idea for her mother. At first, Sarah does not agree. Then, after she hears more information, she changes her mind.

Role-play. Work with a new partner. Complete the conversation with information from Step 1: Organize.

JENNIFER: I went to the family meeting at the Alzheimer's Organization yesterday. They have a new support group. It's a writers' group. Do you want to join it?

SARAH: Jennifer, I have Alzheimer's! How can I be in a writers' group?

JENNIFER: Well, a psychologist started the group. He says this support group really helps people with Alzheimer's because they find . . .

SARAH: Well, I have lost . . .

JENNIFER: . . .

SARAH: . . .

3 FOCUS ON SPEAKING

A VOCABULARY

◀ REVIEW

Work with a partner. Student A, look at this page. Student B, look at Student Activities page 211. Student A, read each sentence. Listen to your partner's response. Does it make sense? If it doesn't make sense, tell your partner, "I don't think that's right."

1. My grandmother has Alzheimer's **disease**.

2. All of our **relatives** are helping her.

3. Sometimes she can't **remember** our names.

4. She looks so **lonely** sometimes.

Switch roles. Listen to Student B. Choose the correct response.

- I know. She was so sad to **lose** her job. She really loved it.

- Yes, but the **members** all help **each other**, too.

- That's true. But she has some clear **memories** of her childhood. She wrote a story about a day when she **got lost** in a park.

- Yes. And then she didn't feel so **lonely**.

◖EXPAND

1 *What do you like to do? Check (✓) **Yes** or **No** for each phrase.*

I Like To:	Yes	No
travel **alone**.	○	○
hang out with my friends.	○	○
do my homework **on my own**.	○	○
walk or jog with a friend.	○	○
study with my friends.	○	○
listen to music **by myself**.	○	○
spend time with my family.	○	○
eat in a restaurant **by myself**.	○	○
go to parties **by myself**.	○	○
go shopping with friends.	○	○
play video games with a friend.	○	○
_____ (your own ideas)	○	○

You can say, "I (don't) like to . . ." to tell someone what you (don't) like. There are also other phrases you can use to say "I (don't) like":

I (don't) enjoy myself
I (don't) have fun   ⎫ when I . . .
I (don't) have a good / great / etc. time ⎭

---

2 *Take turns with a partner. Tell your answers to Exercise 1. Say a whole sentence. Begin with **I (don't) enjoy myself when I . . .**, **I (don't) have fun when I . . .**, or **I (don't) have a good / great / etc. time when I . . .***

Examples

A: I enjoy myself when I *travel alone*. How about you?
B: I don't have a good time when I *travel alone*.

B: I have fun when I *hang out with my friends*. How about you?

A: I have fun when I *hang out with my friends*, too.

A: I don't have a good time when I *study by myself*.

B: I don't have a good time when I *study by myself*, either.

◖ CREATE

Student A, choose three of your partner's answers from Expand. Ask your partner, "Why?" Start like this: **"Why do / don't you like to _____?"**

Student B, answer using one or two (or more!) of the expressions from Review and Expand. Then switch roles.

Example

A: Why do you like to *go to parties* **by yourself**?

B: I like to *go to parties* **by myself** because I like to meet new people. When I *go to parties* together with friends, I **have a good time**, but I don't make new friends.

B: Why do you like to *travel* **with friends**?

A: I like to *travel* **with friends** because I **enjoy myself** when I **spend time with** my friends in a new place. When I *travel* **by myself**, I feel lonely. I **don't enjoy myself**.

B GRAMMAR: *Like to, want to, need to*

When we use the verbs **like**, **want**, and **need** with a second verb, the second verb is in the **infinitive form** (*to* + base form of the verb).

LIKE TO, WANT TO, NEED TO	
1. To form affirmative statements, use **subject + *like(s) / want(s) / need(s)* + *to* + base form of the verb**	**She likes to write** stories. **They need to study** for the test.
2. To form negative statements, use **subject + *don't / doesn't* + *like / want / need* + *to* + base form of the verb**	**She doesn't like to write** stories. **They don't need to study** for the test.
3. To form questions, use **(Why / What) Do / Does / Don't / Doesn't + subject + *like / want / need* + *to* + base form of the verb**	**Does she like to write** stories? **Why do they need to study** for the test?

Take turns with a partner. Student A, read a sentence. Student B, ask a question using the verbs in parentheses. Student A, answer in a full sentence.

Example

A: Ben said, "I can't drive a car anymore. My wife takes me everywhere."

B: (*need / do*) What _____does_____ Ben's wife _____need to do_____ ?

A: (*need / take*) She _____needs to take_____ Ben everywhere.

1. **A:** Herb said, "My wife, Rhoda, was a very successful fashion designer. But now, she can't choose her clothes in the morning."

    B: (*need / do*) What _____ Herb
    _____ do?

    A: (*need / choose*) Herb _____ Rhoda's clothes.

2. **A:** Sarah said, "I have Alzheimer's! I can't join the writers' group!"

    B: (*not / want / join*) Why _____ Sarah
    _____ the writers' group?

    A: (*not / want / join*) Sarah _____ the writers'
    group because _____ .

3. **A:** Joe said, "The writers' group is wonderful. I have fun there."

    B: (*like / go*) Why _____?

    A: (*like / go*) Joe _____ because _____ .

4. **A:** Elsa said, "Sometimes, I can help the other members with their stories. Then I feel so good!"

    B: (*like / do*) What _____?

    A: (*like / help*) Elsa _____ .

5. **A:** Sarah said, "I don't get together with my old friends anymore. I feel lonely."

    B: (*want / make new friends*) Why _____?

    A: (*want / make*) Sarah _____ because _____ .

6. **A:** Jennifer said, "It's very important for people to go to the Alzheimer's Organization. At the family meetings, they can learn how to help their relatives."

    B: (*people / need / go*) Why _____?

    A: (*need / go*) People _____ because _____ .

◀ **PRONUNCIATION:** /ey/ and /ɛ/

1 ⟨CD 7 59⟩ *Listen to the speaker. Are the boldfaced sounds in br**ea**kfast and br**ea**k the same or different?*

I'm really hungry. I didn't have br**ea**kfast. Let's take a br**ea**k and get something to eat.

PRONOUNCING /ey/ AND /ɛ/

/ey/ is the vowel sound in the word *may* /mey/.
Your lips are spread.
Your tongue is in the center of your mouth.

/ɛ/ is the vowel sound in the word *met* /mɛt/.
Your lips are relaxed.
Your tongue is a LITTLE BIT lower and farther back than for /ey/.

2 ⟨CD 7 60⟩ *Listen to the phrases and repeat them.*

/ey/	/ɛ/
1. make a mistake	7. best friends
2. take a break	8. Did you get lost?
3. waves on the water	9. I can't remember.
4. That's great!	10. Try again.
5. always	11. How many?
6. one day last May	12. Go ahead and ask your question.

3 *Jane Oliver asks Dr. Dienstag a question.*

a. ⟨CD 7 61⟩ *Read and listen to Dr. Dienstag's answer on the next page. Don't write anything.*

b. ⟨CD 7 62⟩ *Listen again and write /ey/ or /ɛ/ above the boldfaced syllables on the next page.*

c. *Compare your answers with a partner's. Then listen again to check your answers.*

JANE OLIVER: Dr. Dienstag, I have a **ques**tion, too. How did you **get** the idea /ɛ/   /ɛ/
for the Alzheimer's writers' group?

DR. DIENSTAG: 1. **Well**, I have to **say**, it really wasn't my idea!

2. The idea **came** from a **fa**mous writer **named** Don DeLillo.

3. His mother-in-law had Alzheimer's, and I **met** her.

4. She wanted to re**mem**ber things.

5. But she was for**get**ting more and more **every** **day**.

6. Don DeLillo was looking for a **way** to **help** his mother-in-law.

7. One **day**, he told me his idea about a writers' group.

8. I thought it was a **great** idea.

9. So we decided to work to**geth**er.

d. *With a partner, take turns reading Dr. Dienstag's sentences aloud. Listen to your partner's pronunciation. If you hear a mistake, ask your partner to repeat the word, or check with your teacher.*

4   🔘 *Listen to the conversations and write the words you hear in the blanks. Then practice the conversations with a partner. Be sure to pronounce all the words with /ey/ and /ɛ/ correctly.*

1. **A:** I'm really tired of working.

   B: I am too. **Let's** _____ and **get** some coffee.

2. **A:** Can I ask a **ques**tion?

   B: Absolutely. _____.

3. **A:** What happened? You're really **late**. Did you _____?

   B: **Yes**. I'm sorry. I al**ways** for**get** how to **get** here.

4. **A:** I don't know **a**nyone here. I feel **very** uncomfortable.

   B: Don't worry. You'll _____ fast here. **Every**one is **very** **friend**ly.

(continued on next page)

5. **A:** You told me the **test** was to**day**. But the teacher **said** it's tomorrow.

   B: Sorry. I _____. I thought she **said** to**day**.

6. **A:** Do you want to _____ this week**end**?

   B: That's a **great** idea. How about a movie?

◖ FUNCTION: Interrupting Politely to Ask a Question

When Dr. Dienstag talks to the family group, some of the relatives **interrupt him politely** to ask questions. Look at the boldfaced phrases.

DR. DIENSTAG: The members of my group get together once a week, and they write stories together.

RELATIVE 1: **Excuse me,** did you say they write stories?

DR. DIENSTAG: Yes, they write stories about their memories. Then they read their stories to the group, and we talk about them.

RELATIVE 2: **Sorry, but** my father sometimes doesn't remember my name. How can writing a story help him?

RELATIVE 1: **I'm sorry for interrupting, but** . . .

Here are some useful expressions for interrupting someone politely:

Sorry, (but)	Excuse me,
I'm sorry, (but)	(I'm) sorry for interrupting, but . . .

Work with a partner. Student A, read the sentences on this page. Student B, turn to Student Activities page 212. Student B will interrupt you in sentences 3, 5, and 7.

Conversation 1

1. Do you know the best way to get rid of stress? It's meditation.

3. Yeah. I meditate for twenty minutes a day, and . . .

5. Yeah. I enjoy meditating and it really helps . . .

7. Well, I don't need to take any medicine for my stress, and my meditation group is . . .

9. Yes. We have fun getting together every week.

Switch roles. Respond to Student B's sentences. Where you see a blank, interrupt Student B with a phrase from the box.

Conversation 2

2. How did you do it?

4. _____ what is *Smokenders?* I never heard of it.

6. _____ how did they help you?

8. _____ how do you relax? Do you meditate?

10. That's great! Congratulations!

◖ **PRODUCTION: Presentation**

In this unit, you learned about different groups. ***Now think of a group or club that your classmates will want to join. Make a poster for your group and present it to the class.*** Try to use the vocabulary, grammar, pronunciation, and phrases for interrupting politely from the unit.*

Work in groups of three. Follow the steps.

Step 1: Think of a club that your classmates will want to join, for example, an English conversation club, or a restaurant club (the members have dinner at a different kind of restaurant every week). When you discuss your ideas with your group, try to use expressions for interrupting politely when you want to speak.

Step 2: As a group, make a poster to advertise your club. Make it interesting so your classmates will want to join your club.

---

*For Alternative Speaking Topics, see page 100.

Step 3: Presenters: As a group, give a short presentation to the class. Each person in the group must give some information about the club. Answer these questions in your presentation:

- What is your club called?
- When and where does it meet?
- Why will people **enjoy themselves** in this club?
- Who is it for?
- What do the **members** do?
- Can anyone **join** it?

Tell your classmates that they can interrupt politely to ask questions during the presentation.

Example

STUDENT 1: Hi. We **want to tell** you about our club. It's called "The English conversation club." This club is for people who **have fun when they hang out** with their friends and also **want to practice** their English.

STUDENT 2: Everybody **needs to speak** English more. In our club, you can **have fun when you speak** English!

STUDENT 3: . . .

Listeners: Listen to your classmates' presentations and look at their posters. Use the phrases from Function to interrupt the presenters politely several times!

Step 4: After all the groups have done their presentations, vote on **a)** which group had the best idea for a new club and **b)** which group had the best poster.

ALTERNATIVE SPEAKING TOPICS

Discuss one of the topics. Use the vocabulary and grammar from the unit.

1. Were you ever a member of a group or a club? What kind of group was it? (a study group, a sports team, a drama group, a volunteer group, a hobby group, etc.) Did you make any friends in that group? Did you have a good time? Why or why not? Tell everything you can remember about this group.

2. What's your earliest memory? Work in pairs. Tell your classmate how old you were and what you remember. Then share your memories with the class. Interrupt your classmates politely to ask questions.

RESEARCH TOPICS, see page 218.

UNIT
6
Thinking Young:
Creativity in Business

Picture 1

Picture 2

1 FOCUS ON THE TOPIC

A PREDICT

Look at the pictures. Discuss the questions with the class.

1. What are the co-workers doing in picture 1? How do they feel?

2. What are the same co-workers doing in picture 2? How do they feel?

3. What does "Thinking Young" mean?

Creative people have new and unusual ideas. Sometimes they create or make new things. Children are usually creative when they play. They have many new ideas.

1 *When you were a child, what creative thing(s) did you do? Circle your answers. Then share your answers with three classmates. Ask, "What did you do?"*

a. I created a new game or toy.

b. I created a piece of art (painting, sculpture).

c. I wrote a song or played a musical instrument.

d. I wrote a story or poem.

e. I solved a problem in an unusual way.

f. (something else?) _____

2 *When you were creative, how did you feel? Circle all the words that describe your feelings. Use your dictionary for help.*

a. proud

b. excited

c. happy

d. nervous

e. (another feeling?) _____

C **BACKGROUND** AND **VOCABULARY**

1 CD2 *Read and listen to the information from the business magazine* Fast
2 Company.

Can Your Employees Learn to Be More Creative?
Many Business Owners Say "YES!"

Big companies, like American Express®, Microsoft®, FedEx Kinko's®, and Disney®, want their **employees** to be creative—to think in new and interesting ways. These companies pay billions of dollars for **creativity** classes for their employees.

In some creativity classes, employees play games together in a classroom. In others, they play **exciting** sports together outside the classroom. These activities help employees think in new ways. For example, at the Play Company, a **successful** advertising company, employees go white-water rafting and rock climbing together.

In creativity classes, teachers also give employees important advice:

- Relax. When people relax, they can think better.
- Don't **be afraid to make mistakes**. No one is perfect. **Try to** do your best. Great ideas sometimes come from mistakes.
- Think young! Children are very creative, so we need to think like children sometimes.

Big companies become successful when their employees have new and creative ideas. A successful business **owner** said, "One creativity class can be more valuable than years of **work experience**." Other owners of big companies agree. Creativity classes are great for business.

2 *Circle all of the choices that correctly complete the sentence.*

When employees relax and play games, they can _____.

a. make a lot of money

b. get creative ideas for work

c. feel young again

d. lose their jobs

e. think in new ways

f. feel afraid to make mistakes

3 *Take turns with a partner. Look at the boldfaced words in the magazine article. Student A, read the sentence and choose the correct meaning. Student B, say "Yes, I agree" or "No, I don't think so. I think . . ."*

Example

Employees are (*people who work for a company / people who have no jobs*).

A: Employees are people who work for a company.
B: Yes, I agree.
    OR
A: Employees are people who have no jobs.
B: No, I don't think so. I think employees are people who work for a company.

(continued on next page)

1. Business **owners** are people who (*work for a business / have a company*).

2. A **successful** company is a company that (*makes a lot of money / has many employees*).

3. **Creativity** means having ideas that (*can make a lot of money / are new and different*).

4. When you have **work experience**, it means you (*worked at a job / got a new job*).

5. When you **try to** do something, you (*make an effort to do it / are very good at it*).

6. To **be afraid to** do something means to be nervous and scared because (*something is very boring / something is difficult or different*).

7. When you **make mistakes**, you do something (*the right way / the wrong way*).

8. **Exciting** things (*are a lot of fun / cost a lot of money*).

② FOCUS ON LISTENING

A | LISTENING ONE: K-K Gregory, Young and Creative

GRADUATE SCHOOL OF BUSINESS

SPECIAL LECTURE!
"Personal Creativity in Business"
Guest speaker: K-K Gregory

9:00–11:00
Room 121
Prof. M. Ray

BUS G341
Course

Wristies®, Inc.
P.O. Box 577
Bedford, MA 01730-0577

K-K Gregory
voice 781-275-2223
fax 781-275-8120
e-mail kk@wristies.com
web www.wristies.com

patent pending

CD 2
3 *Listen to the beginning of "K-K Gregory, Young and Creative." Then circle the correct answer.*

1. Who is K-K?
   a. a young company owner
   b. a young business student

2. Why does Professor Ray want K-K to speak to his students?
   a. She's excited to be there.
   b. The students can learn from her.

3. What will K-K talk about?
   a. her high school
   b. her business

◖ LISTEN FOR MAIN IDEAS

1 *CD 2*
4 *Listen to K-K Gregory. Write **T** (true) or **F** (false). Correct the false sentences.*

fingers
thumb
hand
wrist
wristie

_____ 1. K-K started her business when she was 17 years old.

_____ 2. Wristies keep your fingers warm.

_____ 3. K-K's mother helped her make the first pair of Wristies.

_____ 4. K-K's mother didn't have any business experience.

_____ 5. K-K thinks it's good to try to do new things.

2 *Go back to Section 2A, Question 3. Was your answer correct?*

CD 2
⑤ *Listen again. Two answers are correct. Cross out the incorrect answer. Read the two correct answers.*

1. When you wear Wristies, _____.

    a. ~~your thumbs are covered~~
    b. your wrists are warm
    c. you can move your fingers

2. K-K made the first pair of Wristies _____.

    a. because she didn't have gloves
    b. on a snowy day
    c. when she was 10 years old

3. K-K's friends _____.

    a. really liked their Wristies
    b. wanted to sell their Wristies
    c. wore their Wristies every day

4. K-K thought about starting a business _____.

    a. because her friends suggested it
    b. after her mother said it was a good idea
    c. when she made the first pair of Wristies

5. When K-K started the Wristies company, _____.

    a. her mother helped her
    b. her mother had a store
    c. she had a few problems

6. People can buy Wristies _____.

    a. in many stores
    b. on the Internet
    c. at the supermarket

7. When K-K went on a TV shopping show, _____.

    a. she was very successful
    b. she sold 2000 pairs of Wristies
    c. she was nervous and excited

8. K-K's advice to the business students is _____.

    a. be creative
    b. do new things
    c. start your own business

◀ MAKE INFERENCES

Listen to the excerpts from Listening One. Circle the best answer to complete each sentence.

CD 2

6 Excerpt One

1. The students probably think _____.
   a. K-K did something very funny
   b. K-K did something very unusual
   c. K-K is 10 years old

CD 2

7 Excerpt Two

2. K-K's mother probably helped her because she wanted K-K to _____.
   a. make a lot of money
   b. get some business experience
   c. do something creative and exciting

CD 2

8 Excerpt Three

3. The students are surprised that K-K _____.
   a. was so successful
   b. was on TV
   c. was nervous

◀ EXPRESS OPINIONS

1 *Many people e-mail K-K to tell her why they like to wear Wristies. Here are a few examples from her website. Try to think of other people who can wear Wristies. Write your ideas on the list.*

```
http://www.wristles.com
```

1. musicians who perform outside or in cold rooms
2. people who work at "drive-thru" windows of fast-food restaurants
3. motorcyclists
4. artists
5. fishermen (and women)
6. mail carriers

7. _____

8. _____

9. _____

10. _____

11. _____

HOME

ABOUT US

ORDER

CONTACT US

2 *Answer the questions.*

1. "K-K's mother made an excellent decision. It's a very good idea for a child to have a business." Do you agree or disagree with this statement? Explain your opinion.

2. Do you ever buy things on the Internet? On TV shopping shows? From catalogs? Are these ways better than shopping in stores? Why or why not?

B **LISTENING TWO: A Business Class**

Professor
Michael Ray,
Stanford
University

1 CD2 *Listen to Professor Ray's lecture. Write **T** (true) or **F** (false). Correct the false sentences.*

_____ 1. K-K made something that people needed.

_____ 2. K-K listened only to her mother.

_____ 3. Children are not afraid to do new things.

_____ 4. Adults think it's OK to make mistakes.

_____ 5. If you want to be creative, don't be afraid to make mistakes.

_____ 6. Meditation can help the students remember their childhood.

_____ 7. The students in Professor Ray's class will try to sleep.

_____ 8. The students will remember a time when they were afraid.

2 *Listen again to Professor Ray and follow his directions. When you are finished, tell your story to a partner. Then discuss your stories with the class.*

C INTEGRATE LISTENINGS ONE AND TWO

◀ STEP 1: Organize

Professor Ray told his students that K-K had three important lessons to teach them:

1. Find something that people need.

2. Listen to other people.

3. Don't be afraid to do something new.

Look at K-K's story. Decide which lesson business students can learn. Circle the number of the lesson in the right column. Sometimes there is more than one lesson.

K-K'S STORY	WHAT BUSINESS STUDENTS CAN LEARN		
1. K-K was wearing gloves, but her wrists were very cold. That's when she had an idea.	①	2	3
2. Her friends wore their Wristies every day. They liked them a lot.	1	2	3
3. K-K's friends told her, "You can sell your Wristies."	1	2	3
4. K-K's mother had no business experience, but she thought a business was a great idea.	1	2	3
5. K-K and her mother talked to a lot of people, asked a lot of questions, and learned a lot.	1	2	3
6. K-K went on a TV shopping show to sell Wristies. She was very nervous, but it was exciting. She sold 1,000 pairs of Wristies.	1	2	3

Nathan, a student in Professor Ray's business class, has some questions about K-K's talk. He took notes in his notebook, but he made some mistakes.

Role-play. Work with a partner. Student A, you're Nathan. Use your notes to tell Professor Ray what you wrote in your notebook. Student B, you're Professor Ray. Correct Nathan's mistakes. Then explain what we can learn from K-K's experience. Complete the conversation with information from Step 1: Organize. Take turns being A and B.

1. K-K got the idea for Wristies because her <u>fingers</u> were cold.
2. Her friends <u>didn't</u> wear their Wristies.
3. K-K's <u>mother</u> said, "Sell your Wristies."
4. K-K's mother had <u>a lot of business experience.</u>
5. K-K talked to <u>one or two</u> people. She <u>didn't</u> learn a lot.
6. K-K sold <u>100</u> pairs of Wristies on a TV shopping show.

Example

NATHAN: Well, K-K said that she got the idea for Wristies because her **fingers** were cold, right?

PROF. RAY: No, her wrists were cold, not her fingers. She needed something to make them warm. So, we learn that you have to find something that people need.

③ FOCUS ON SPEAKING

Ⓐ VOCABULARY

❙ **REVIEW**

Work in pairs. Read the story about another young and creative business owner, Brent Simmons. Fill in the blanks with words from the box. Then take turns reading the story aloud.

afraid	exciting	made mistakes	successful
creative	experience	owner	try

When Brent Simmons was 10 years old, he knew everything about computers. Whenever his friends or relatives had problems with their computers, they came to Brent for advice. When other people said, "It's impossible to fix this computer," Brent was never

**Brent Simmons,
"Computer Doctor"**

_____ to look for a new way to fix it.
       1.

Sometimes he _____, and he had to start
               2.

again. But in the end, he usually found a new and very

_____ way to fix the computer.
    3.

　　Brent loved to fix computers. So, when he was 14, he started his own

company. Brent is the _____ of the company. He made more
                4.

than $50,000 a year when he was still in high school, so from the beginning,

his business was very _____. "Sometimes people come to me
                 5.

with difficult computer problems," says Brent. "I always _____
                                6.

to help them. When I can find the problem and fix it, they are so happy. For

me, that's an _____ feeling.
           7.

　　Brent is a young man with a lot of business _____.
                                   8.

1  *Read and listen to the paragraph about creativity in business.*

When employees take creativity classes, they **increase** their **creativity**. Then they can **come up with** many new and unusual ideas. When employees are stressed out, they can't be creative. So some companies have free meditation classes for their employees. Meditation **makes them feel** calm and relaxed. This is an important **perk** for some workers. They save money because it's free, and they **save time** because they don't need to leave work. Some companies have another interesting perk. They give their employees scooters to ride inside their building. The employees have fun, and they can **get around** very quickly. Some companies put large white boards on the walls. Employees write their new ideas on these boards. Then everyone discusses his or her ideas. These are some of the cool **features** that are now popular in many creative offices.

2 *Work with a partner. Student A, read a sentence in the left column. Student B, read the correct response from the right column. Switch roles for Conversation 2.*

Conversation 1: The Play Company

1. Why does the Play Company have creativity classes?

2. Did you know that at the Play Company, there are no tables or chairs in the meeting rooms?

3. After a one-hour meeting, the employees had 50 new ideas!

4. Employees at the Play Company say that they feel so relaxed at work.

a. Wow! How did they **come up with** so many new ideas in such a short time?

b. The Play Company wants to **increase** employees' **creativity** in meetings.

c. The Play Company really tries to **make** its employees **feel** comfortable.

d. Really? The Play Company's office has some very unusual **features**.

Conversation 2: Fun Ideas, Inc.

5. Listen to this. The employees at Fun Ideas, Inc. get three free meals a day, free haircuts, and free massages!

6. These perks really help employees.

7. The employees use scooters to go from one place to another.

8. Fun Ideas, Inc. wants everyone to have fun and relax. When people relax, they are more creative.

e. True. They help them to **save time**.

f. That's great. You can't be creative when you're stressed out.

g. Wow! Those are unusual **perks** to give employees.

h. Really? That's a strange way to **get around** an office!

CREATE

Interview two classmates using the questions. When it is your turn to answer the question, use the words from Review and Expand.

1. How do you **try** to increase your **creativity**?

2. What is **exciting** about your job or classes?

3. What are you **afraid** of?

4. What do you do when you make a **mistake**?

5. How do you **try to** be **successful**?

B GRAMMAR: *There is / There are, There was / There were*

1 *Read the conversation. Follow the directions.*

PROFESSOR RAY: Are there any more questions?
STUDENT: Yes. Were there any problems in the beginning?
K-K: Yeah, there were a few problems! For example, business was very slow at first because there weren't any other people in my company. There was only one person—me! Now there are three employees.

a. Find and underline *there are, there was, there were,* and *there weren't* in the conversation.

b. Which ones talk about the present? Which ones talk about the past? Which one is singular?

c. Find and underline *Are there* and *Were there.*

1. Use **there is** or **there are** to describe a situation in the present.

There is + *a* + singular count noun
There is + non-count noun

Use the contraction **There's** in speaking or informal writing.

There are + plural count noun

There is a website.
There is information about Wristies on the website.

There's a website.
There's information on the website.

There are many places where you can wear Wristies.

2. Use **there was** or **there were** to describe a situation in the past.

There was + *a* + singular count noun
There was + non-count noun
There were + plural count noun

There was a problem in the beginning.
There was snow on the ground.
There were problems in the beginning.

3. To form a negative statement, add the contraction **n't**.

There are**n't** any more questions.
There were**n't** many employees.

4. For questions, put **is / are** or **was / were** before **there**.

Are there any questions?
Was there a problem yesterday?
When **was there** a problem?

In **yes / no** questions, use *a* with singular nouns, and **any** with plural nouns and non-count nouns.

Is there a problem?
Were there any problems?
Was there any snow?

---

2 Read the interview with Andy Stefanovich, co-founder of the Play Company. Fill in the blanks using **there** + a form of the verb **be**. Use the contraction **there's** when possible.

ANDY: Welcome to Play Company! Please come in.

INTERVIEWER: Wow! This office has some very unusual features!

ANDY: Yes, when people come to our office for the first time, they're

             usually surprised.

INTERVIEWER: Is this your meeting room?

ANDY: No, _____ any meeting rooms at Play. This is a
             1. (neg.)
"playroom."

INTERVIEWER: A playroom?

ANDY: Sure. We learn to be creative from children. And children play!

So this playroom is where we come up with all our new ideas.

_____ a meeting in this playroom one hour ago.
        2.
Let's look around.

INTERVIEWER: But . . . _____ any tables or chairs in this room.
           3. (neg.)

_____ really a business meeting here? Are you sure?
        4.
It looks like children were playing here. _____ balls
                               5.
and children's toys on the floor, and _____
                                  6.
pictures and pieces of paper on the floor and walls!

ANDY: Those are some ways that we try to increase our creativity.

Boring meetings give people boring ideas. Play meetings are

exciting! At play meetings, the employees play! And

_____ a table in the room because we like to
        7. (neg.)
write on special material on the walls! Do you see that?

_____ a special camera in each playroom. The
        8.
camera photographs everything that we write on the walls.

OK, now look over there. _____ a list on that wall
                 9.
of all the new ideas from the meeting. Let's see . . .

_____ ten people in this room for one hour, and
        10.
now _____ 50 new ideas on this list.
        11.

INTERVIEWER: This is really an unusual place to work!

ANDY: Yeah. Working here is a lot of fun!

3 *Now read the interview aloud with a partner. Switch roles and read it again.*

C SPEAKING

◀ **PRONUNCIATION of TH:** *think, this*

How many words with "th" can you find in this sentence?

We sold 333,333 pairs of Wristies.

PRONOUNCING *TH* SOUNDS

Put the tip of your tongue between your teeth.

This is the most important part of the pronunciation of the "th" sounds.

Blow out air to make the sound. Keep the tip of your tongue between your teeth.

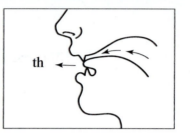

The "th" sound in *this*, *these*, and *then* is a voiced sound. The vocal cords vibrate.
The "th" sound in *think*, *three*, and *thousand* is a voiceless sound. The vocal cords do not vibrate.

The tip of the tongue is between the teeth for both sounds.

---

1 CD 2 🔘 *Read the sentences and underline every word that has a "th" sound. Then read the sentences aloud to a partner. Be sure to pronounce all the "th" sounds correctly. Listen to the sentences to check your pronunciation.*

1. They're long gloves with no fingers.

2. There's a hole for the thumb.

3. Some people wear them outside; others wear them inside.

4. They all wore them every day.

5. So then I thought, "I can sell these things!"

6. My mother didn't know anything about business.

7. A lot of stores sell them, and there's also a website.

2 Work with a partner. Student A, ask each question. Student B, answer each question using a word from the box. Student A, listen to your partner's answer. Say "That's right" or "I don't think that's right." If you don't think it's right, discuss the answer. Take turns being A and B.

anything	thinks	~~thousand~~
mother	thought	thumb

Example

A: How many Wristies did K-K sell on TV?

B: She sold a ____thousand____!

A: ____That's right____.

1. **A:** Why does K-K like business?

   B: She _____ it's exciting.

   A: _____.

2. **A:** Who helped K-K a lot?

   B: Her _____ did.

   A: _____.

3. **A:** Did K-K know a lot about business when she was 10?

   B: No, she didn't know _____!

   A: _____.

4. **A:** Did K-K's mother like the idea of selling Wristies?

   B: Yes, she _____ it was a good idea.

   A: _____.

5. **A:** Why do Wristies have a little hole?

   B: That's for the _____.

   A: _____.

When people tell us new information, we usually show our interest. The expression we use depends on whether the news is very surprising or not.

INTERESTING OR GENERAL INFORMATION	
Uh-huh ...	**K-K:** Don't be afraid to try something new. **PROF. RAY:** *Uh-huh ...*
Really ... That's interesting ...	**K-K:** So, I asked my mother about it, and she thought it was a great idea. So she helped me to start my company.
Oh, really?	**PROF. RAY:** *Oh, really?*
SURPRISING OR UNUSUAL INFORMATION	
Wow!	
That's so interesting!	**K-K:** There are a lot of places where you can wear them. **PROF. RAY:** *That's so interesting!*
That's great! / wonderful! That's amazing! / incredible!	**K-K:** And that's how I made the first pair of Wristies. **PROF. RAY:** *That's great!*

Practice reading the reactions in the chart above. Then role-play the conversation about Google's World Headquarters with a partner. Student A, read the sentence. Student B, respond with the best expression from the chart above. Take turns being A and B. Try to use all of the expressions.

1. **A:** Did you know that Google employees wear jeans to work?

   B: _____

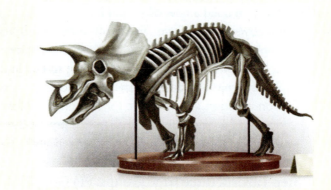

2. **A:** Listen to this! There is a real dinosaur skeleton[1] on the first floor of Google's office!

   B: _____

3. **A:** Google employees play roller hockey[2] twice a week in the parking lot.

   B: _____

4. **A:** Did you know that Google employees can bring their dogs to work?

   B: _____

5. **A:** Google bought its building in California for $319 million.

   B: _____

6. **A:** There are giant red and blue rubber balls all over Google's office.

   B: _____

7. **A:** At Google, three or four employees work in one area with no walls.

   B: _____

8. **A:** In the Google office, there is an exercise room that is open 24 hours a day.

   B: _____

---

[1]**skeleton:** all the bones in an animal or person

[2]**roller hockey:** a sport played on the street in which players use long curved sticks to try to hit a ball into a goal; the players wear Rollerblades®

In this activity, you will role–play a business meeting at Google. Google wants to build a new office in Philadelphia, PA. The company wants to help its employees be creative. Today, office designers from Google are meeting with employees from Google's New York and California offices. The designers want to know which features of each office to use in the new Google office. You will play the role of a designer or an employee. Try to use the vocabulary, grammar, pronunciation, and language for reacting to information from the unit.*

Step 1: Form three large groups: (1) Google office designers, (2) Employees from Googleplex, Google's California office, and (3) Employees from Googleplex East, Google's New York office.

Step 2: Prepare for a role play.

- Google office designers: Prepare questions to ask the employees from the two offices.

Example

Is there anything unusual on the first floor of the building?

How many cafeterias or restaurants are there?

- Employees from Googleplex, CA: Read the list of features and perks of your office.

GOOGLEPLEX, CALIFORNIA

an indoor rock climbing wall (for exercise)	10 cafeterias
an outdoor sand volleyball court	an exercise room
2-lap swimming pools	a game room
car washes	a 4-star restaurant
glass walls dividing the offices inside	a hair salon
a video game room	a sushi bar
a massage room	a doctor's office
funny posters on the walls	
special bus service from employees' homes to work (free)	

PERKS

free chef-prepared food all day
free massages
skateboards
free sports training

*For Alternative Speaking Topics, see page 122.

- Employees from Googleplex East, NY: Review the list of features and perks of your office.

GOOGLEPLEX EAST, NEW YORK

glass walls dividing offices
big red rubber exercise balls
balloons with happy faces all around the building
a game room with foosball, air hockey, a billiards table
whiteboards on the walls—employees can write any ideas
  they have, and other employees can add their ideas

Razor® scooters
electric train sets
massage chairs
dog play area

PERKS

free massages
video games, foosball, air hockey
employees' dogs (but not cats) can come to work with them

Step 3: Form small groups with one student from each of the large groups. Now each group has at least one (1) Google office designer, (2) employee from Googleplex, CA, and (3) employee from Googleplex East, NY.

Step 4: Each group will have a meeting to choose the features and perks for the new Google office. Students can refer to their lists. Begin the meeting like this:

DESIGNER: Could you tell me about the features of *Googleplex* California?
CALIFORNIA: OK. There is a massage room in our office. When employees are stressed out, they can . . .
DESIGNER: Does that help to increase creativity?
CALIFORNIA: Sure! When employees feel stressed out, they can't come up with creative ideas.
NEW YORK: Yes, I agree. We don't have a massage room, but . . .

Step 5: Each group will write the features and perks it chose on the board. As a class, select the features and perks for the new Google office.

ALTERNATIVE SPEAKING TOPICS

Discuss one of the topics. Use the vocabulary and grammar from the unit.

1. Many companies want their employees to be more creative. These companies have unusual activities for employees. Here are some of the activities. Which are good ways to increase creativity? Which are not? Check (✓) the boxes. Explain your reasons to the class.

	IT'S A GOOD IDEA.	IT'S NOT A GOOD IDEA.	I'M NOT SURE.
Doing exciting sports together		✓	
Studying music	✓		
Sometimes working at home			✓
Playing games together		✓	
Learning how to meditate	✓		

2. Do you know a successful business owner? What kind of business does this person own? Why is this person successful?

RESEARCH TOPICS, see page 219.

Planting Trees for Peace

1 FOCUS ON THE TOPIC

A PREDICT

Look at the picture. Complete the activity and discuss the questions with the class.

1. Look at the drawing. Write each word on the line next to the object it describes.

branch	leaves	roots	seeds	trunk
field	river	seedling	soil	wood

2. How do trees help people?

3. Are trees good for the soil? Why or why not?

A

B

1.

1.
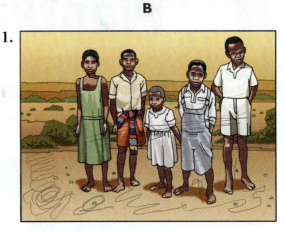

2.

2.

3.

3.

Work in a small group.

1. Look at the pictures in column A. In poor countries, how do people get food? Say one or two sentences about each picture.

2. Look at the pictures in column B. In poor countries, what happens when all of the trees in one place are cut down? Say one or two sentences about each picture.

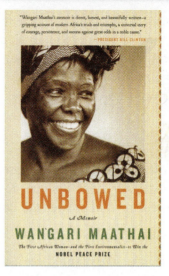

1  *Read and listen to the story of Wangari Maathai's life.*

Excerpts from "The Life of Wangari Maathai" (1940–)

My childhood

I grew up in Kenya, in a small village in the countryside. We had a river with clean water and many trees. We **planted** corn, beans, bananas, and sweet potatoes in our beautiful green fields. The people in my village were poor, but we were never hungry.

My love of nature

My mother taught me about my Kikuyu[1] culture. She **encouraged** me to love nature. The Kikuyu people say, "Everything in the environment is from God, so we must always **take care of** it—the **land** we live on, the trees all around us, and our beautiful clean rivers. We must never **destroy** anything in nature."

Changes in my country

I studied at a university in the U.S. for five years. But when I came back to Kenya, everything was very different. There was a new government. It was not a **democracy**. The new president did many bad things to our people. And the people had no **political power**. When I returned to my village, I was so **shocked**. There were no more trees! **Without** trees, the soil became dry, and the rain washed it away. The women couldn't plant vegetables in the dry land. Our river dried up, too. The women in my village walked for many hours to find clean water and wood for cooking.

(continued on next page)

---

[1]**Kikuyu:** the name of a cultural group in Kenya

Changes in my village

In Kenyan villages, women must get the food for their families. But without trees, there wasn't enough food or water. Nobody had money to buy food. So the people became hungry. Many children became sick. They couldn't go to school. Some children died. The women didn't know what to do about this terrible situation. I wanted to help, and I had an idea. I decided to **speak out** to the women in my village.

2 *Work with a partner. Student A, read the sentence with the underlined vocabulary. Ask the question about the meaning. Student B, choose the correct meaning and answer the question. Take turns.*

Example

1. **A:** We <u>planted</u> corn, beans, bananas, and sweet potatoes in our beautiful green fields. What does *planted* mean?

   B: *Planted* means <u>put seeds into the ground</u> .

      a. put seeds into the ground
      b. used plants for food

2. **A:** My mother <u>encouraged</u> me to love nature. What does this sentence mean?

   B: It means _____.

      a. my mother tried to teach me to love nature
      b. my mother didn't think nature was important

3. **A:** We must always <u>take care of it</u>—the land we live on, the trees all around us, and our beautiful clean rivers." What does *take care of it* mean?

   B: *Take care of it* means _____.

      a. thank God for it
      b. keep it in good condition

4. **A:** We must always take care of it—<u>the land</u> we live on, the trees all around us . . ." What does *the land* mean?

   B: *The land* means _____.

      a. the ground under our feet
      b. the street near our house

5. **A:** We must never <u>destroy</u> anything in nature. What does *destroy* mean?

   B: *Destroy* means _____.
       a. change; make different
       b. hurt; kill

6. **A:** There was a new government. <u>It was not a democracy.</u> What does this sentence mean?

   B: This sentence means _____.
       a. the people chose the government
       b. the people didn't choose the government

7. **A:** The people had no <u>political power</u>. What does *political power* mean?

   B: *Political power* means _____.
       a. ability to change the government
       b. ability to make money

8. **A:** When I returned to my village, I was so <u>shocked</u>. What does *shocked* mean?

   B: *Shocked* means _____.
       a. very surprised and worried
       b. very interested and excited

9. **A:** <u>Without</u> trees, the soil became dry . . . What does *without* mean?

   B: *Without* means _____.
       a. there were some
       b. there weren't any

10. **A:** I decided to <u>speak out</u> to the women in my village. What does *speak out* mean?

    B: *Speak out* means _____.
        a. speak freely and openly
        b. speak quietly to a few people

② FOCUS ON LISTENING

A LISTENING ONE: Wangari Maathai and the Green Belt

🔊 *CD 2 13* *Listen to the beginning of the recording. Then choose the correct answer.*

1. I am listening to _____. (Circle the answer.)
   a. a conversation
   b. a TV show
   c. a history class

2. What will you probably learn more about? Check (✓) your ideas.

   _____ different kinds of trees in Africa   ✓ poor villages in Africa

   _____ the government in Kenya   _____ Wangari's family

   _____ the Nobel Peace Prize[1]   _____ problems in the environment

LISTEN FOR MAIN IDEAS

1 *CD 2 14* *Read the events in Wangari Maathai's life. Listen to the entire TV show. As you listen, number the events in the correct order.*

Timeline: Wangari Maathai's life from 1970–2004

Part One (1–4)

_2_ Wangari started the Green Belt. She taught women about the environment.

_1_ People in Wangari's village lost their trees and became hungry.

_____ Many African women planted trees and their lives got better.

_____ Wangari encouraged women in her village to plant trees.

Part Two (5–8)

_4_ The president tried to destroy the Green Belt, but he couldn't.

_____ The government said, "No."

_3_ The Green Belt asked the government for help.

_2_ Wangari said, "Kenya needs a democracy."

---

[1] **Nobel Peace Prize:** an important award given to a person who has worked to bring peace to the world

_____ Wangari Maathai became a member of the government.

_____ Kenyans chose a new democratic government.

_____ Wangari Maathai received the Nobel Peace Prize.

2 _Now go back to Section 2A, Question 2, on page 128. Were your ideas correct?_

◖ **LISTEN FOR DETAILS**

CD 2
15
Listen to the TV show again. Circle the correct answer to complete each sentence.

1. Wangari said, "Planting a tree is very _____."
   a. easy   **b.** difficult

2. After the women planted trees, they _____.
   a. felt better   **b.** had wood

3. Women _____ planted thousands of trees.
   a. in Wangari's village   **b.** all over Kenya

4. When a woman planted a tree, the Green Belt gave her some _____.
   a. money   **b.** new seedlings

5. The Green Belt couldn't help everyone in Kenya. They needed help from the _____.
   a. people   **b.** government

6. The president's friends cut down the trees because they wanted to _____.
   a. plant coffee fields   **b.** destroy the Kenyans' lives

7. Wangari said that Kenya _____ a democratic government.
   a. had   **b.** needed

8. Almost everybody in Kenya wanted Wangari to _____.
   a. be in the government   **b.** be in the Green Belt

Listen to the excerpts from the TV show. Choose the correct answer. Then compare your answers with your classmates'.

CD 2
🔘16 **Excerpt One**

1. Why were the women so excited after they planted new trees?
   a. They could get fruit and wood from the trees right away.
   b. They did something important to change their lives.

CD 2
🔘17 **Excerpt Two**

2. Why were the Green Belt members shocked that the government didn't help them?
   a. The government promised to help them.
   b. The government's job is to help its people.

CD 2
🔘18 **Excerpt Three**

3. Why did the Green Belt members want a new government?
   a. The president didn't care about his friends.
   b. The president didn't care about the poor people in his country.

CD 2
🔘19 **Excerpt Four**

4. What does Wangari mean when she says, "We plant the seeds of peace"?
   a. When people have enough food, they don't have to go to war.
   b. When people plant seedlings, they feel peaceful.

◀ **EXPRESS OPINIONS**

Discuss the questions with a small group.

1. Wangari Maathai is also famous as a leader for women's rights[1]. How did she help women? Why was her work important for women in her country?

2. The Nobel Peace Prize Committee looks for someone "who is an example for us to follow" and "who gives us hope for the future." Why was Wangari a good choice for the Nobel Peace Prize?

3. Many countries have a special day for planting trees. Does your country have one? Why do you think countries have this day? Is it a good idea?

B | **LISTENING TWO: Rigoberta Menchu, a Mayan Leader**

Sara and Ruth are taking a history class. Each student has to give a presentation to the class about an important woman in the twentieth century.

---
[1]**women's rights:** the same political and legal rights for women and men

Rigoberta Menchu

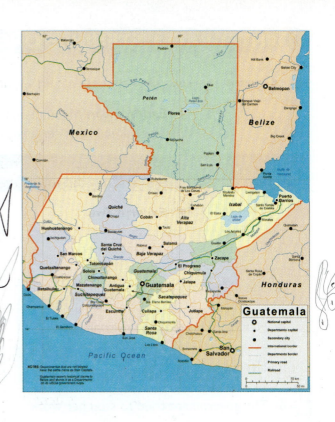

Guatemala

1 CD 2 *Listen to the conversation between Ruth and Sara. Write **T** (true) or **F** (false).*
20 *Correct the false information.*

_____ **1.** Most Mayan people in Guatemala have equal rights.[2]

_____ **2.** Rigoberta works to help poor people and women.

_____ **3.** Rigoberta was the first Guatemalan person to win the Nobel Peace Prize.

_____ **4.** Rigoberta stopped going to school when she was eighteen.

_____ **5.** Guatemala had a democratic government at that time.

_____ **6.** Rigoberta couldn't stay in Guatemala.

_____ **7.** In Mexico, Rigoberta continued working for democracy.

_____ **8.** Rigoberta said that war is sometimes necessary.

_____ **9.** Rigoberta lives a violent[3] life.

2 *Compare your answers with a partner's and then with your other classmates'.*

---

[2]**equal rights:** the same rights for everyone
[3]**violent:** using force to hurt someone

STEP 1: Organize

1 How are Wangari Maathai and Rigoberta Menchu similar? How are they different? Read each sentence and check (✓) the correct column.

	WANGARI	RIGOBERTA	BOTH
1. She lived in the countryside.	✓	✓	✓
2. Her culture is important to her.	✓		✓
3. She did not have an education.		✓	✓
4. Her work helped the environment.	✓		
5. Her work helped the Mayan people.			
6. The government tried to stop her work.			✓
7. She wanted equal rights for the Mayan people and all women.		✓	✓
8. She believed that planting trees could bring peace.	✓		

2 Compare your answers with your classmates'.

STEP 2: Synthesize

Ruth and Sara did their presentations in their history class. Now, their professor wants the class to compare Wangari Maathai and Rigoberta Menchu.

Role-play. Work with a partner. You are students in the history class. Student A, talk about how Wangari and Rigoberta are **similar** or **the same**. Student B, talk about how Wangari and Rigoberta are **different**. Complete the conversation with information from Step 1: Organize and Listenings One and Two.

A: Well, Wangari and Rigoberta are similar in a lot of ways. Wangari came from a poor family, and Rigoberta did, too.
B: Right, but Wangari is from . . . , and Rigoberta is from . . .

A VOCABULARY

◀ REVIEW

Work with a partner. Student A, look at this page. Student B, look at Student Activities page 213. Student A, read each sentence below aloud. Listen to your partner's response. If it doesn't make sense, tell your partner, "I don't think that's right."

1a. Wangari <u>always told the women in the Green Belt, "The president can't stop us! We will win!"</u>

2a. The president of Kenya tried to <u>stop</u> the Green Belt Organization.

3a. The police <u>hurt</u> Wangari.

4a. The president of Kenya put Wangari in <u>prison</u>.

Switch roles. Listen to Student B. Complete your responses with a word or phrase from the box.

beat (someone) up	destroy	jail	violence
democracy	encouraged	political	without

5b. I know. She told the Mayan people, "We can change the government _____ fighting."

6b. That's true. She didn't want people to use _____.

7b. That's right. She wanted a _____.

8b. You're right. She became an important _____ leader in Guatemala.

EXPAND

1 *Read the story about Wangari Maathai. Fill in the blanks with a verb from the box that has the same meaning as the words in parentheses.*

care about 2	fighting for 5	spoke out
~~dreamed of~~	3 had courage	were against

In 1989 President Moi decided to cut down all the trees in Uhuru Park,

Nairobi's only park. He wanted to build a tall office building there. He also

_____ **dreamed of** _____ building a very tall statue of himself next to the
　　 1. (had a strong wish)

building.

The people in Nairobi _____ the president's plan.
　　　　　　　　　　　　2. (did not like)

They said, "The president doesn't _____ us. He only
　　　　　　　　　　　　　3. (think we are important)

thinks about himself." Wangari Maathai agreed. She said, "President Moi

cannot destroy Uhuru Park. Then she and other members of the Green Belt

went to Uhuru Park, and they _____ against the
　　　　　　　　　　4. (expressed their opinions about)

president's plan. They explained why the park was so important, especially to

poor people in Nairobi.

President Moi sent the police to beat up Wangari and the other women,

but the women _____; they refused to leave the park.
　　　　　5. (were not afraid)

They said, "The people of Nairobi need this park. We are

_____ the people of Nairobi, and for a clean
　　6. (supporting)

environment." Many people agreed with the women. In the end, President

Moi had to forget about his building and his statue. The women won the

fight!

2 🔊 *Now listen to the passage and check your answers.*
　CD2
　21

Work with a small group. Take turns asking and answering the questions. Use the underlined vocabulary in your answers.

1. Wangari Maathai said that women in politics need to <u>have courage</u>. Why did she say this? Do you agree?

2. Who <u>speaks out</u> about the problems of poor people where you live? Do most people <u>care about</u> poor people's lives?

3. Is it possible to <u>fight for</u> a <u>political</u> change <u>without violence</u>? Can you give any examples of people who did this?

4. Were you ever <u>against</u> a government plan? What was it? Tell what happened.

5. Martin Luther King, Jr. <u>fought for</u> <u>equal rights</u> for African American people in the U.S. Dr. King <u>dreamed of</u> a day when all American people could be "brothers."

What do you <u>dream of</u> for your country? <u>Democracy</u>? <u>Equal rights</u>? A clean environment? Something else? Tell about your dream.

B GRAMMAR: Simple Past Tense

Wangari Maathai told this story when she spoke at the United Nations in 2005.

1 *Read the story and underline all the verbs that tell about the past. Then answer the questions on the next page.*

WANGARI MAATHAI: I <u>learned</u> this story from a professor in Japan. I think it has an important lesson for us:

A hummingbird

There was a big fire in the forest, and all the animals started to run away. They said, "We can't do anything. The fire is too big." They waited for some bigger animals to put out the fire. Then they saw a little hummingbird. The hummingbird decided, "I will help to put out this fire." So the hummingbird flew to the river, picked up one little drop of water, returned to the forest, and put it on the fire. The hummingbird saw that the first drop of water did not put out the fire, but he continued flying to the river and back. The other animals laughed at him. "What are you doing? Did you put out the fire?" they asked with a laugh. And the little hummingbird answered, "I'm doing what I can."

So, now I say to you, let us be hummingbirds. Let us do what we can.

1. Which past tense verbs are regular (end in *-ed*)?

a. *learned*   f. looksed

b. Studied   g. _____

c. caused   h. opened

d. recognized   i. closed

e. explaked   j. walked

2. Which past tense verbs are irregular (do not end in *-ed*)?

a. Put   d. cut

b. run   e. came

c. became

3. Find a past tense verb in the negative form. _____

4. Find a question in the past tense. _____

SIMPLE PAST TENSE	
1. Use the simple past tense to talk about actions completed in the past.	
To form the past tense of regular verbs, add **-ed** to the base form of the verb.	Wangari talk**ed** to many women.
If the base form **ends in e, add only -d:** encourage → encourag**ed**	She encourag**ed** them to plant trees.
If the base form **ends in a consonant + y, change y to i and add -ed:** study → stud**ied**	She stud**ied** in the U.S.
If the base form **ends in consonant-vowel-consonant, double the final consonant and add -ed:** stop → sto**pped**	Rigoberta sto**pped** going to school.

	Base Form	Simple Past
2. Many verbs have irregular past tense forms.	become	**became**
	do	**did**
NOTE: The simple past tense of *be* is *was* or *were*.	feel	**felt**
	fly	**flew**
	go	**went**
	have	**had**
	hear	**heard**
	know	**knew**
	make	**made**
	put	**put**
	say	**said**
	see	**saw**
	speak	**spoke**
	tell	**told**
	understand	**understood**

3. To form a negative statement, use *didn't* + base form

People **didn't have** enough food.

4. To ask *yes/no* questions, use

Did + subject + base form

Did she **win** the Nobel Peace Prize?
  Yes, she won the Nobel Peace Prize.
  Yes, she did.

5. To ask *wh-* questions, use
Wh- word + *did* + subject + base form

NOTE: If you do not know the subject of the question, use
Who or What + past tense verb
(Do not use *did*.)

When did she **win** the Nobel Peace Prize?

Who was the first native person to win the Nobel Peace Prize?
  Rigoberta Menchu was the first native person to win the Nobel Peace Prize.
  Rigoberta Menchu was.

2 *Read the conversation and fill in the blanks with the simple past tense of the verbs in parentheses. Then practice the conversation with a partner.*

Eleanor Roosevelt: A Fighter for Human Rights

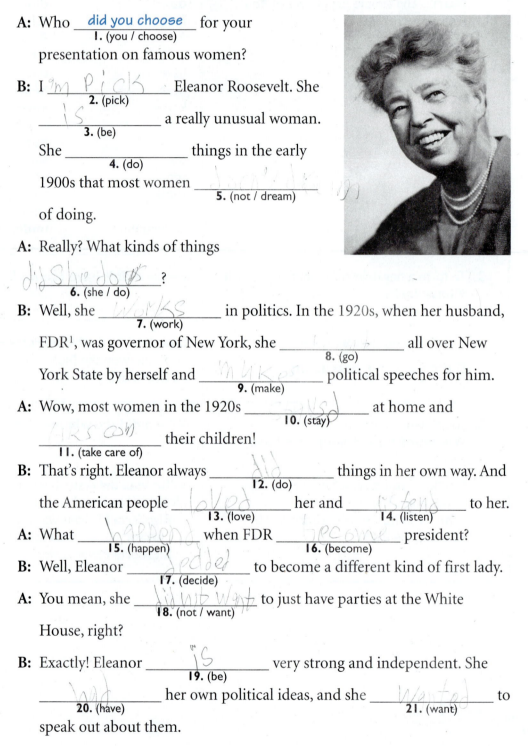

A: Who _____did you choose_____ for your
     1. (you / choose)
presentation on famous women?

B: I ___m Pick___ Eleanor Roosevelt. She
     2. (pick)
___is___ a really unusual woman.
     3. (be)
She _____ things in the early
     4. (do)
1900s that most women _____
     5. (not / dream)
of doing.

A: Really? What kinds of things
___did She do___ ?
     6. (she / do)

B: Well, she ___works___ in politics. In the 1920s, when her husband,
     7. (work)
FDR[1], was governor of New York, she _____ all over New
     8. (go)
York State by herself and ___makes___ political speeches for him.
     9. (make)

A: Wow, most women in the 1920s _____ at home and
     10. (stay)
___took can___ their children!
     11. (take care of)

B: That's right. Eleanor always _____ things in her own way. And
     12. (do)
the American people ___loved___ her and ___listen___ to her.
     13. (love)   **14. (listen)**

A: What ___happend___ when FDR ___become___ president?
     15. (happen)   **16. (become)**

B: Well, Eleanor ___decided___ to become a different kind of first lady.
     17. (decide)

A: You mean, she ___did not want___ to just have parties at the White
     18. (not / want)
House, right?

B: Exactly! Eleanor ___is___ very strong and independent. She
     19. (be)
___had___ her own political ideas, and she ___wanted___ to
     20. (have)   **21. (want)**
speak out about them.

---
[1]**FDR:** Franklin Delano Roosevelt, the 32nd president of the United States

A: What _____ about?
  22. (she / speak out)

B: Well, she _____ that every person ___*had*___ an
  23. (believe)   **24. (have)**

equal right to a good education and a good job. She especially

___*cared about*___ women and children. And she ___*traveled*___ all
  25. (care about)   **26. (travel)**

over the world to help poor people.

A: What ___*Eleanor do*___ after FDR ___*die*___ ?
  27. (Eleanor / do)   **28. (die)**

B: Well, she _____ working! In 1945 she ___*begin*___ to
  29. (not / stop)   **30. (begin)**

work for the United Nations. She ___*help*___ to write the
  31. (help)

Universal Declaration of Human Rights. All her life, Eleanor

___*fight for*___ equal rights for people all over the world.
  32. (fight for)

C SPEAKING

◖ PRONUNCIATION: *-ed* endings

The *-ed* ending is sometimes pronounced as a new syllable and sometimes as a new sound. Listen to your teacher read the sentences.

> The women in Wangari's village <u>planted</u> trees because they <u>hoped</u> for a better future.

> Then they <u>encouraged</u> women in other villages to plant trees.

Look at the underlined verbs. Is the *-ed* ending a new syllable or a new sound?

PRONOUNCING *-ED* ENDINGS	
1. If the last sound in the base verb is /d/ or /t/, **-ed** is pronounced as a new syllable: /ɪd/ or /əd/.	/ɪd/ Wangari Maathai plant**ed** seven trees near her house. /ɪd/ They decid**ed** to ask the government for help.

(continued on next page)

2. After other verbs, the **-ed** ending is pronounced as a new sound, not a syllable:

a. If the last sound in the base verb is /**p**/, /**f**/, /**k**/, /**s**/, /**ʃ**/, or /**tʃ**/, **-ed** is pronounced /**t**/. (See the phonetic alphabet on page 238.)

b. After all other verbs, the **-ed** ending is pronounced /**d**/.

/t/
Wangari work**ed** with the Green Belt to help the environment.

/d/
She explain**ed** the connection between trees and peace.

/d/
The president tri**ed** to stop the Green Belt.

1 🎧 ᶜᴰ ² 22 *Listen to the words. Circle the correct **-ed** ending.*

1. /t/ /d/ /ɪd/   4. /t/ /d/ /ɪd/   7. /t/ /d/ /ɪd/

2. /t/ /d/ /ɪd/   5. /t/ /d/ /ɪd/   8. /t/ /d/ /ɪd/

3. /t/ /d/ /ɪd/   6. /t/ /d/ /ɪd/   9. /t/ /d/ /ɪd/

2 🎧 ᶜᴰ ² 23 **a.** *Read and listen to the sentences about Eleanor Roosevelt's life. Look at the underlined verbs. Is **-ed** pronounced /t/, /d/, or /ɪd/? Write your answers above the verbs.*

/d/
_____ After her parents died, Eleanor <u>lived</u> with her aunt.

/ /
_____ Her lessons <u>helped</u> Eleanor many times later in her life.

/ /
_____ Eleanor always <u>remembered</u> Marie Souvestre's lessons.

___1___ Eleanor Roosevelt had a sad childhood.

/ /
_____ Eleanor <u>loved</u> her school and her teacher, Marie Souvestre.

/ /
_____ Marie Souvestre <u>wanted</u> her students to be strong and independent.

/ /
_____ Both of her parents <u>died</u> when she was very young.

/ /
_____ Then her aunt <u>decided</u> to send her to a girls' school in England.

b. The sentences about Eleanor Roosevelt's life are not in order. Work with a partner to put the sentences in order. Write numbers (2–8) in the blanks to show the correct order. Check your answers with the class. Then practice telling the story with your partner.

3 Work in small groups to tell the story of Rigoberta Menchu's life. Use the subjects given and the past tense of the verbs in parentheses. One person starts the story and the other members of the group continue the story. Pronounce the past tense correctly. (Use irregular past tense verbs when necessary.)

Rigoberta Menchu (She)

a. (not finish) elementary school.

b. (stop) going to school to help her family.

c. (continue) to study on her own, after work.

d. (join) a political group when she was a teenager.

e. (want) to help poor workers.

The government

f. (decide) to destroy the political group.

g. (kill) everyone in Rigoberta's family.

Rigoberta (She)

h. (leave) Guatemala.

i. (go) to Mexico.

j. (work) with other Guatemalans to bring democracy to Guatemala.

k. (help) many people.

l. (win) the Nobel Peace Prize for her work.

When we want to say that one person's experience was similar to another person's experience, we can use a short form.

THE SIMPLE PAST	
1. With two affirmative statements: Tell the information about one person. If the verb is **be**, use **was** or **were** + **too** to tell about the second person.	Rigoberta was from the countryside, and Wangari was from the countryside.
She **was, too**. They **were, too**.	Rigoberta was from the countryside, *and Wangari* **was, too**.
With other verbs, use **did** + **too** She **did, too**.	Wangari fought for democracy, and *Rigoberta* **did, too**. OR **A:** Wangari fought for democracy. **B:** Rigoberta **did, too**.
2. With two negative statements: Tell the information about one person. If the verb is **be**, use **wasn't** or **weren't** + **either** to tell about the second person.	
She **wasn't either**. They **weren't either**.	Wangari wasn't afraid to speak out, and *Rigoberta* **wasn't either**. OR **A:** Wangari wasn't afraid to speak out. **B:** Rigoberta **wasn't either**.
With other verbs, use **didn't** + **either** She **didn't either**.	Rigoberta didn't use violence, and *Wangari* **didn't either**. OR **A:** Rigoberta didn't use violence. **B:** Wangari **didn't either**.

Work with a partner. Take turns reading one fact from the chart and responding to it.

Example

A: Wangari was from Africa.
B: The Green Belt women were, too.
A: Rigoberta wasn't from Africa.
B: Eleanor Roosevelt wasn't either.

	WANGARI MAATHAI	GREEN BELT WOMEN	RIGOBERTA MENCHU	ELEANOR ROOSEVELT
Country	was from Africa	were from Kenya	was from Guatemala	was from the U.S.
Childhood	was from a poor family	were from poor families	was from a poor family	wasn't from a poor family
Beliefs	didn't care when people said bad things about her didn't use violence	didn't use violence	didn't use violence	didn't care when people said bad things about her didn't use violence
Accomplishments	wrote a book fought for equal rights won the Nobel Peace Prize	fought for equal rights	wrote a book won the Nobel Peace Prize	wrote a book fought for equal rights

In this unit, you learned about three important women—Wangari Maathai, Rigoberta Menchu, and Eleanor Roosevelt. ***In this activity, you are going to play the role of one of these women.*** Try to use the vocabulary, grammar, pronunciation, and language for expressing similarities from the unit.*

Step 1: Divide the class into three groups: Group A—Wangari Maathai, Group B—Rigoberta Menchu, and Group C—Eleanor Roosevelt.

Step 2: As a group, talk about your person's life. Be sure that every student in the group knows all the information. Look back at the unit to check any information you need. Then write four questions that your person can ask the other two important women about their lives. Every person in the group must write all four questions.

Step 3: Make new groups with at least one person from Group A, Group B, and Group C. Take turns telling about "your" life (as Wangari, Rigoberta, or Eleanor). Use "I . . ." Answer any questions that your partners ask you.

When your partners are speaking, listen very carefully. If one person tells about an experience, and you had the same experience, tell him/her immediately, using "too" or "either".

---

*For Alternative Speaking Topics, see page 146.

WM:	Hi, I'm Wangari Maathai. I'm from Kenya.
RM AND ER:	Hi Wangari.
WM:	About 30 years ago, I started an organization called the Green Belt.
ER:	What did the Green Belt do?
WM:	We planted trees all over Kenya.
ER:	Did you enjoy your work for the environment?
WM:	Yes, I did. But then I became more political. Kenya wasn't a free country . . .
RM:	Guatemala wasn't either.
WM:	So I started to fight for democracy.
RM:	I did, too.

ALTERNATIVE SPEAKING TOPICS

Work with a partner. Choose topic 1 or 2. Tell your partner about this person. Use past and present tenses. Use the questions below each topic to help you.

1. Rigoberta Menchu and Eleanor Roosevelt had very unhappy childhoods. But later, they both became strong and successful people. They turned their sadness into strength. Think of other famous people and people you know. Who is another person who turned sadness into strength?

   - What is the person's name?
   - Is he or she a famous person, or someone you know?
   - What kind of sadness did this person have?
   - How did this person change his or her life? (How did the person change sadness into strength?)

2. Wangari Maathai, Rigoberta Menchu, and Eleanor Roosevelt were all important leaders in their parts of the world. Who was an important leader (man or woman) in your part of the world? Tell everything you know about this person.

   - What is the person's name?
   - What country was she/he from?
   - What kind of leader was she/he? (political, environmental, etc.)?
   - What did she/he speak out about or fight for?

Listening Activity

*Listen to your partner describe the person he or she chose. Ask your partner questions. Where possible, use phrases to show similarity (**He did too**, **She was too**, etc.).*

RESEARCH TOPICS, see page 219.

UNIT
8
Driving You Crazy

①FOCUS ON THE TOPIC

Ⓐ PREDICT

Look at the picture. Discuss the questions with the class.

1. What is happening in the photograph?
2. How do the people in the photograph feel?

1 *Write the correct word or phrase from the box on the line next to its definition.*

| honk | lane | pay attention | signal | tailgate |

_____ **1.** to put the blinker on in a car; to show another driver that you are going to turn

_____ **2.** to listen or watch something carefully

_____ **3.** to make a loud noise with a car horn

_____ **4.** to drive too close to the car in front of you

_____ **5.** parts of a road separated from another part by lines

2 *Read the sentences. They all describe driving problems. Write the number of each problem under the picture it describes.*

1. The driver is talking on the phone and not paying attention.

2. The car is passing in the wrong lane.

3. The car is turning without signaling; the other driver is honking the horn.

4. The truck is tailgating the car.

   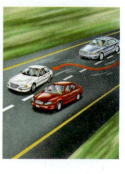

_____   _____   _____   _____

3 *Work with a partner. Discuss the questions. Then share your answers with the class.*

1. What other driving problems can you think of?

2. Some people are afraid to drive. Why?

3. Some people become angry when they drive. Why?

1 🎧 *Read and listen to the blog about driving problems. Pay attention to the boldfaced words.*

---

http://theroadrageblog.com

HOME

COMMENT

ABOUT US

CONTACT US

I Hate Driving (June 9)

I really hate driving these days. More and more people are driving—to work, to school, to their families' homes. So the roads and highways are **crowded** with all these people in their cars. I know most drivers are **polite**. They think about other drivers, and they are careful. But some drivers are not polite at all. These **rude** drivers think only about themselves. They are usually in a hurry, and they don't care about other people on the road. It's especially bad at **intersections**, where two or more roads meet. Sometimes I see drivers crossing intersections too quickly, and they have accidents. People get **injured**. That's why I hate driving.

Comments (June 12)

(1) I agree with you about rude drivers. Why are drivers today so rude? I think it's because in your car, other people don't know you, and you don't know them. You feel **anonymous**, so you don't care what you do. You don't care if you make other people feel angry or uncomfortable, so you don't **control** the way you act.

—Jenn

(2) You're right about feeling anonymous. But I think another reason for rude driving is stress. Many people are stressed out because of problems at work or traffic. When people feel nervous or worried, they sometimes drive badly. They have accidents.

—Chris

(3) That's true. My friend was really stressed out last year, and she had three car accidents. Three in one year! She had to go to **traffic school**. She learned to think about other drivers and to be more polite on the road. She's a better driver now.

—Deepa

---

2 *Choose the correct word to complete the sentence.*

The writers on this blog agree that there are many _____ drivers on the road today.

    a. careful   **b.** polite   **c.** bad

3 *Circle the correct definition of the underlined word to complete each sentence.*

1. If a road is <u>crowded</u>, there are _____.

   a. many cars
   b. few cars

2. <u>Polite</u> drivers think about _____.

   a. other drivers on the road
   b. where they are going

3. A <u>rude</u> driver cares only about _____.

   a. himself/herself
   b. other drivers

4. At an <u>intersection</u>, two roads _____.

   a. are next to each other
   b. cross each other

5. When a person is badly <u>injured</u>, he or she needs to _____.

   a. relax
   b. see a doctor

6. To be <u>anonymous</u> means that no one _____.

   a. knows you
   b. likes you

7. To <u>control</u> your behavior means to _____.

   a. think about and change it
   b. enjoy it and continue it

8. <u>Traffic school</u> is a place where people learn how to _____.

   a. drive carefully
   b. drive a car

② FOCUS ON LISTENING

A LISTENING ONE: Road Rage

CD 2
25
You will hear an instrutor speaking at traffic school. He is speaking about road rage, a serious driving problem. Listen to the beginning of the traffic school lesson. Read the questions on the next page and discuss the answers with the class.

1. What is road rage?

2. Why is road rage dangerous?

3. When the traffic school students hear the stories about road rage, how will they feel? Check (✔) your ideas.

_____ tired   _____ stressed out   _____ nervous

_____ scared   _____ angry   _____ happy

◀ LISTEN FOR MAIN IDEAS

CD2
26
Listen to two true stories of road rage. The two speakers are John and Marie. What did each person do? Check (✔) the correct answers.

	John	Marie
1. got angry	○	○
2. got scared	○	○
3. changed lanes	○	○
4. tailgated another car	○	○
5. drove into a parking lot	○	○
6. honked at another driver	○	○

◀ LISTEN FOR DETAILS

CD2
27
*Listen again. Write **T** (true) or **F** (false).*

_____ 1. Twelve hundred (1,200) people are injured every year because of road rage.

_____ 2. John forgot to signal when he changed lanes.

_____ 3. A driver followed John.

_____ 4. The driver hit John's car with his truck.

_____ 5. Marie was driving a red sports car.

_____ 6. Marie passed another driver.

_____ 7. Road rage happens because drivers feel stressed out.

_____ 8. Fifty percent (50%) of American highways are very crowded.

_____ 9. You can learn to control other drivers.

_____ 10. Listening to the radio can make you angry.

◖ MAKE INFERENCES

Listen to the excerpts from Listening One. Circle the best answer to each question.

CD2
28 **Excerpt One**

1. Why does John ask the instructor, "Do you know how it feels when you're really tired?"
   a. John thinks the instructor is tired.
   b. John is always really tired.
   c. John was very tired when he was driving home from work.

2. How did the truck driver feel?
   a. angry
   b. stressed out
   c. nervous

CD2
29 **Excerpt Two**

3. How did Marie feel while she was driving?
   a. angry and scared
   b. angry and surprised
   c. angry and sad

4. How does Marie feel now?
   a. still surprised
   b. still angry
   c. still scared

CD2
30 **Excerpt Three**

5. According to the instructor, what is true about the past?
   a. There was less traffic.
   b. There were smaller cars.
   c. There was more road rage.

6. According to the instructor, what can we do to stop road rage?
   a. control our anger
   b. control bad drivers
   c. control traffic

◀ **EXPRESS OPINIONS**

*Read the statements. Do you agree or disagree? Mark each one **A** (Agree) or **D** (Disagree). Then compare your answers with a partner's. Give reasons for your opinions.*

_____ **1.** John is not a very good driver.

_____ **2.** The truck driver was wrong to act the way he did.

_____ **3.** Listening to music is a good way for a driver to control anger.

_____ **4.** All drivers should learn about road rage before they get a license.

_____ **5.** Men have more road rage than women.

_____ **6.** Some people are often angry. They are the people who have road rage.

B LISTENING TWO: Driving Phobia

Road rage is one driving problem. Another driving problem is fear. A very strong fear is called a phobia. People with a driving phobia are afraid to drive. Some people with phobias get help from psychologists. The psychologists help them to understand and control their fear.

CD 2
🔵31 *Allen has a driving phobia. Listen to the conversation between Allen and his psychologist. Then circle the correct answer to complete each sentence.*

1. Allen is afraid of _____.

  a. driving a truck
  b. losing control of the car

2. Allen is afraid that _____.

  a. he will hit a truck
  b. a truck will hit him

3. The psychologist tells him to think of other things _____.

  a. that he is afraid of
  b. that he does well

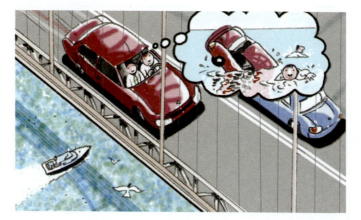

(continued on next page)

4. The psychologist tells him to _____.

    a. look straight ahead

    b. look at the water

5. In the end, Allen feels _____.

    a. very happy that he crossed the bridge

    b. a little unhappy because he didn't cross the bridge alone

C INTEGRATE LISTENINGS ONE AND TWO

◀ STEP 1: Organize

Look at the chart. Work with a partner to complete the chart with information from Listenings One and Two.

	DRIVING PROBLEMS	WHERE THEY GOT HELP	WHAT THEY LEARNED
John	1. driving when tired 2. 3.	traffic school	Don't drive when you're tired. Don't forget to signal. It's dangerous.
Marie	1. 2. 3.		
Allen	1.		

Role-play. Work in groups of four. You are John, Marie, Allen, and a student in traffic school. You are speaking to a group of traffic school students. The students are asking you questions about your driving problems. Answer the students' questions using information from Step 1: Organize. Switch roles for each question.

Question 1:

STUDENT: What was your biggest driving problem?

JOHN: Well, . . .
MARIE: My problem was . . .
ALLEN: I couldn't . . .

Question 2:

STUDENT: How did you feel? What did you do?

JOHN: I felt . . .
MARIE: I was very . . .
ALLEN: Well, . . .

Question 3:

STUDENT: What did you learn about driving better?

JOHN: . . .
MARIE: . . .
ALLEN: . . .

Question 4:

STUDENT: What is your advice for other drivers?

JOHN: . . .
MARIE: . . .
ALLEN: . . .

3 FOCUS ON SPEAKING

A VOCABULARY

REVIEW

1 *A police officer is speaking to a group of new drivers. She is answering their questions. Read the conversation and fill in the blanks with the words from the box. You will not use all of the words.*

anonymous	injured	polite	rude
control	intersection	psychologist	traffic school
crowded	phobias	road rage	

POLICE OFFICER: Do you think driving is more dangerous these days?

NEW DRIVER 1: I don't know.

PO: Well, guess what: It is. Our roads are getting more and more _____.
1.

ND 1: Wait a minute. Why is that dangerous?

PO: It's not when drivers are polite, when they pay attention to other drivers and give them time. But it's very dangerous when drivers are _____!
2.

ND 2: What do you mean? How is that a problem?

PO: How's that a problem? Well, they just don't care about other drivers. That's why we see more and more road rage. Drivers honk their horns every minute. They're totally stressed out—maybe because of their problems.

ND 1: What kinds of problems?

PO: I don't know . . . work problems, home problems, whatever. The main thing is this: you can't _____ other drivers.
3.

ND 2: You can't?

PO:	No! You can't change their bad driving. But do you know who you can control?
ND 1:	Who?
PO:	You! That's who. You can control only your own driving.
ND 2:	I guess that makes sense.
PO:	Sure it does. And watch out for bad drivers—they're all around you. Some are rude. Others are afraid. They have _____ . **4.**
ND 1:	They have what?
PO:	Fears, or phobias. You know, they're scared of driving. One day last year, I saw a man with a driving phobia. He was driving so slowly, I couldn't believe it. And when other people honked at him, he got even more scared. Some drivers need a psychologist. They really do.
ND 2:	I see.
PO:	So, here's my advice. Don't drive when you're angry, when you feel road rage. Don't drive when you're thinking about something else. Always be careful, especially when you cross a busy _____ of two or more streets. **5.**
ND 1:	Hold on. Don't drive when I'm angry? But what if I have a bad day at work?

PO:	Then leave your car at work. Find another way to get home. If you drive when you're angry, other people can get _____ because of your road
	                                                            6.
	 rage. And if you see a problem on the road, call us. The police won't ask for your name. You can be _____ . OK? Drive safely. I don't want to
	                                       7.
	 see you in _____ !
	                        8.

2 CD2 32 *Now listen to the audio. Check your answers to Exercise 1.*

3 *Role-play the conversation with a partner.*

1 A traffic student is describing his experience in traffic school. Read the passage.

> "Traffic school was OK. The teacher was funny. I can't really **complain** about him, but I'm still **frustrated** about my **ticket**. It cost me a lot of money. The **officer** didn't care that I was speeding because I was stressed out that day. I was having trouble with money and work. It was a really bad time for me. I asked him to **give me a break**, to let me go. But he **refused**. I guess he was just doing his job."

2 Circle the correct answer to complete each sentence.

1. When we <u>complain</u>, we say what _____.
   a. we like
   b. we don't like

2. To be <u>frustrated</u> is to be _____ about something.
   a. angry
   b. happy

3. Drivers get a <u>ticket</u> when they _____.
   a. go to traffic school
   b. break the law

4. An <u>officer</u> works _____.
   a. for the police
   b. in an office

5. When we <u>give someone a break</u>, we _____.
   a. make him pay for his mistakes
   b. forget about his mistakes

6. To <u>refuse</u> is to say _____.
   a. no
   b. yes

Work in pairs. Discuss your experiences on the road—as the driver or the passenger. Take turns answering the questions and completing the sentences.

1. When do you get <u>frustrated</u> on the road?

2. Do people <u>complain</u> about your driving? Do you <u>complain</u> about other people's driving?

3. I <u>refuse</u> to . . . when I'm walking/driving/riding a bus.

4. One time, I got a <u>ticket</u> because . . .

5. When I see a <u>police officer</u>, I . . .

6. I want police officers to <u>give me a break</u> when . . .

B GRAMMAR: Simple Past and Past Progressive

1 *Look at the sentences. Then answer the questions.*

1. John was driving home from work. He forgot to signal.

2. Marie got angry at another driver. He was driving a red sports car.

a. What are the verbs? Underline them.

b. How are the verbs similar? How are they different?

SIMPLE PAST	
Use the simple past to describe finished actions or situations.	
1. We use the simple past to talk about a specific time in the past: **last year, last month**, **yesterday,** and so on.	1. Marie and John **had** driving problems **last year**.
2. Some simple past verbs are regular. Add **-ed** to these verbs (*followed, honked*).	2. A truck driver **followed** John. She **honked** her horn at him.
3. Some simple past verbs are irregular (*got, became*).	3. John **got** scared. Marie **became** angry at another driver.

PAST PROGRESSIVE

Use the past progressive to describe an action that was happening but not finished at the same time that another finished action happened.

1. Use **when** or **while** to show that one action was happening at the same time that another finished action happened. Use the **simple past** with **when** for the finished action. Use **while** before the unfinished action.	**1.** [unfinished] **While** John **was driving** home from work, [finished] he **turned** without signaling. [unfinished] John **was driving** home from work **when** [finished] he **turned** without signaling.
2. Use **while** to show that two unfinished actions were happening at the same time. Use the **past progressive** with **both verbs**.	**2.** [unfinished] **While** John **was driving**, the truck driver [unfinished] **was following** him. [unfinished] **While** Marie **was driving**, she [unfinished] **was honking** her horn.
3. To form the past progressive, use the past tense of the **be verb and add -ing to the main verb.** I was driving. You were driving. He was driving. They were driving. She was driving We were driving.	**3.** Many drivers **were honking** their horns while I **was driving** home last night.

2 *Read the short stories. Each one tells a true story of road rage. Complete the sentences with the correct verb tense. Use the simple past or past progressive.*

A. A few years ago, an insurance company _____ drivers in
1. (study)
Calgary, Canada. The insurance company _____ that many
2. (learn)
drivers in Calgary _____ rude. For example, while they
3. (be)
_____, they often _____ very angry and
4. (drive) **5. (get)**
_____ other drivers.
6. (tailgate)

B. I _____ to New Delhi, India, last year. When I
7. (travel)
_____ in New Delhi, I _____ the bus every day. I
8. (be) **9. (ride)**
_____ very scared while I _____ the bus in New
10. (feel) **11. (ride)**
Delhi. The bus driver _____ his horn at all the other drivers
12. (honk)
while he _____ very fast.
13. (drive)

C. My friend _____ the Philippines last summer. At that time,
14. (visit)
a man _____ a woman while they _____ about a
15. (injure) **16. (fight)**
parking space.

3 *Work with a partner. Student A, interview Student B about a driving problem.
Student B, tell your own true story or a story based on one of the pictures.
Student A, listen and take notes. Then switch roles.*

Student A, ask the questions.

1. What kind of problem did you (or the driver) have?
2. What were you doing when it happened?
3. What were other people doing?
4. What happened next?
5. What finally happened?

4 *Use your notes to prepare a short speech about your partner's driving problem. Use **when** and **while**. Then give your speech to the class.*

Example

My partner is Victor. Two years ago, Victor was late for work. There was a lot of traffic while he was driving on the freeway. He tried to drive faster. He was going very fast when a police car stopped him. The police officer gave him a ticket. While the police officer was writing the ticket, Victor was thinking about work. When he checked his watch, he saw that it was getting later and later. He finally arrived at work. It was bad. He had a ticket, and he was in trouble with his boss.

C SPEAKING

PRONUNCIATION: *Thought Groups*

Longer sentences are broken into shorter, meaningful groups of words. The shorter groups are called *thought groups*. The words in a thought group are pronounced together.

CD2
33 *Listen to a driver's explanation of an accident. What words does the driver put together?*

DRIVER: The driver on my left turned into my lane, without signaling. I tried to stop, but I couldn't. I hit him.

THOUGHT GROUPS	
Long sentences are pronounced in thought groups.	
Thought groups express information. They are often grammatical phrases like prepositional phrases.	He stopped in the middle of the road.
There are different ways to say the groups of words in a sentence.	He stopped in the middle of the road.
Say the words in a thought group together.	He stopped in the middle of the road.
To join one thought group to another thought group, hold (lengthen) the end of the first thought group before you start the next thought group.	He turned without signaling. hold I tried to stop, but I couldn't. hold

1 CD 2 *Listen to the cell phone conversation and repeat the sentences. Use the*
  🔘 *underlines to group words together. Then practice the conversation aloud*
  34 *with a partner.*

A: I think I'm lost.

B: Are you still on the highway?

A: No. I got off at Exit 9, just a minute ago.

B: Is there a stop sign in front of you?

A: Behind me. I just went through it.

B: Is there a gas station ahead of you?

A: I think so. Down the road on the left.

B: You're not lost. Make a right turn at the gas station. You'll see my house.

2 *Read the sentences. Draw lines to show thought groups. Then compare your*
thought groups with a partner's. You might have different groups. Practice saying
the sentences with your partner. Lengthen the end of the first group before you
start the next group.

   1. In South Africa, cars drive on the left.

   2. In the United States, cars drive on the right.

   3. It's not easy for Americans to drive in South Africa.

   4. Sometimes they have accidents because everything seems different.

3 *Work with a partner. Use the information in Exercise 2 and the information*
below to make true sentences about driving in South Africa and in the United
States. It may help you to draw the roads and cars. When you explain driving in
the two countries, group words together.

Example

In South Africa, faster cars keep to the right on divided highways. In the
United States, faster cars keep to the left on divided highways.

In (South Africa / the United States) . . . .

   faster cars keep to the (right / left) on divided highways.

   slower cars keep to the (left / right) on divided highways.

   you should pass other cars on the (right / left).

   you should look to the (right / left) when you make a (left / right) turn.

   you should look to the left and right when you make a (left / right) turn.

1 *People have different ways of thinking about situations, or different points of view. Read the conversation between a psychologist and a driving school instructor. Look at the boldfaced expressions.*

PSYCHOLOGIST: Well, **don't you think** people can change if somebody helps them?

DS INSTRUCTOR: I think some people will never change. They will always be bad drivers.

PSYCHOLOGIST: **Wait a minute.** People can change if they want to.

DS INSTRUCTOR: **I disagree.** Some people keep making the same mistakes over and over again.

PSYCHOLOGIST: Maybe that's because they don't want to change.

DS INSTRUCTOR: **What about this?** Some people promise to change, but they never do.

PSYCHOLOGIST: **Well, I still think** they can change if they want to.

Useful Expressions for Giving Different Points of View

- Don't you think . . . ?
- Hold on.
- I disagree.
- I don't see it that way.

- Wait a minute.
- Well, I still think . . .
- What about this?

---

2 *Work in groups of four. Take turns reading the statements aloud. Practice expressing different points of view about the statements.*

Example

Women drive better than men.

STUDENT 1:   <u>Wait a minute</u>. That depends on the person. Some women are terrible drivers.

STUDENT 2:   <u>I don't see it that way</u>. Women are usually more careful than men.

STUDENT 3:   <u>Don't you think</u> that's a problem sometimes? If you're too careful, you can have accidents.

STUDENT 4:   <u>I disagree</u>. It's very important to be careful. <u>What about this?</u> Teenage boys have a lot of accidents. They're not careful when they drive . . .

1. Men drive better than women.

2. People under 21 should not drive.

3. People over 65 should not drive.

4. Drivers with road rage problems should lose their driver's licenses.

5. Drivers with road rage problems should go to prison for 20 years.

◖ PRODUCTION: Case Study

> In this unit, you learned about road rage. Parking rage is another driving problem. In crowded cities with a lot of traffic, it can be very difficult to find parking spaces. Drivers sometimes fight with each other and also with the parking control officers. ***In this activity, you will read a case study based on a true story of parking rage. Discuss the case and decide on the best punishment for the driver.*** Try to use the vocabulary, grammar, pronunciation, and language for expressing different points of view from the unit.*

Follow the steps.

Step 1: Work in groups of three or four. Read about a case of parking rage.

On March 25, a 23-year-old college student parked her car in a no-parking area in front of an office building. She was taking her laptop computer to a computer business for repair[1]. The driver spent five minutes inside the building. When she returned to her car, a parking control officer

[1]**repair:** the act of fixing something that is not working

*For Alternative Speaking Topics, see page 167.

was standing at her car. He was writing her a ticket. When the driver complained about the ticket, the officer told her that there was a public parking garage down the street. The driver said that she went to the garage first but it was full. She asked the officer to give her a break, but the officer refused. While the officer was writing the ticket, the driver became angry. She yelled and pushed the officer against her car three times.

The driver is a full-time college student. She was frustrated because her laptop wasn't working and she needed to do a lot of schoolwork. Last year, four anonymous people complained about the officer. They said the officer was rude and didn't care at all about drivers' problems.

Step 2: Now discuss the case. In your conversation, answer these questions.

   a. What happened?

   b. Which person do you agree with (the driver or the officer)?

Step 3: What punishment should the driver receive? Choose from the list below.

   a. She should get a ticket (decide how much money the driver should pay).

   b. She should lose her driver's license.

   c. She should go to traffic school for six weeks.

   d. She should go to prison for 1–5 years.

Step 4: Present your decision to the class. Make sure that each member of your group has a chance to speak. Answer your classmates' questions.

Step 5: Listen to the other groups speak. Ask questions about their decision.

ALTERNATIVE SPEAKING TOPICS

Discuss one of the topics. Look at the information in the chart and the graphs to answer the questions. Use the vocabulary and grammar from the unit.

Car Accident Deaths by Age Group and Year				
Age Group	2002	2003	2004	2005
16–20	6,299	6,030	5,924	5,699
41–45	3,472	3,568	3,427	3,480
56–60	1,792	2,028	2,068	2,213
Over 65	6,387	6,391	6,213	6,207

Source: FARS 1996–2004 (Final), 2005 (ARF)

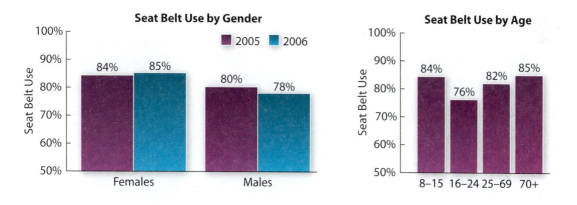

Seat Belt Use by Gender
2005 2006
Females: 84% 85%
Males: 80% 78%

Seat Belt Use by Age
8–15: 84% 16–24: 76% 25–69: 82% 70+: 85%

1. Which two groups of drivers are involved in the most deadly car accidents?

2. Who uses seat belts more—males or females? Who uses seat belts more—older people or younger people?

3. What group of drivers seems to be the most dangerous? Why do you think this is true?

4. What can we do to solve the problem of dangerous drivers?

RESEARCH TOPICS, see page 220.

UNIT 9

Only Child— Lonely Child?

Family A

Family B

1 FOCUS ON THE TOPIC

A PREDICT

Look at the pictures. Discuss the questions with the class.

1. Read the title of the unit. What does it mean? What is an *only child*?

2. How does the child in family A feel? Why?

3. How do the children in family B feel? Why?

169

1 *Walk around the room. Ask four classmates the questions. Complete the chart.*

QUESTIONS	ANSWERS

1. Do you have any brothers or sisters?
(If NO, go to question 2.)
(If YES, ask these questions:)
 	
a. How many brothers and sisters
(= siblings) do you have?
    Classmate 1: _____
    Classmate 2: _____
    Classmate 3: _____
    Classmate 4: _____
	No, I don't. / Yes, I do.
	(If NO, go to question 2.)
	(If YES, use these answers:)
	
	I have _____ brother(s) and _____ sister(s).
	    Classmate 1: _____
	    Classmate 2: _____
	    Classmate 3: _____
	    Classmate 4: _____

b. How old is he / she?
OR
How old are they?
    Classmate 1: _____
    Classmate 2: _____
    Classmate 3: _____
    Classmate 4: _____
	My brother / sister is _____ (years old).
	OR
	One brother / sister is _____ (years old), and
	one brother / sister is _____ (years old).

c. Are you the oldest child in your family, the youngest child, or the middle child?
    Classmate 1: _____
    Classmate 2: _____
    Classmate 3: _____
    Classmate 4: _____
	I'm the _____ child in my family.

QUESTIONS	ANSWERS
2. (If NO:) **a.** When you were a child, did you ever feel lonely? Did you want a sibling? Classmate 1: _____ Classmate 2: _____ Classmate 3: _____ Classmate 4: _____	**2.** (If NO:) Yes, I did. / No, I didn't.
b. Do you want a sibling now? Why or why not? Classmate 1: _____ Classmate 2: _____ Classmate 3: _____ Classmate 4: _____	Yes, I do. / No, I don't.
c. Your question: _____ Classmate 1: _____ Classmate 2: _____ Classmate 3: _____ Classmate 4: _____	_____

2 *Tell your teacher about your results.*

How many students:

don't have any siblings? _____

have one sibling? _____

have two siblings? _____

have more than two siblings? _____

1 *Lisa and Jules Conner are the parents of an only child. They started a new magazine for single-child families. Read their magazine article. Choose the correct word for each blank. Compare your answers with a partner's.*

    Only Child is the first magazine _____ for families with just one child. We
                     1. (enough / especially)

started this magazine because we want to *speak out* about our wonderful families! Many people

think that only children are lonely because they don't have _____. We know that
                                     2. (a baby / siblings)

this is not true. We can spend a lot of time with our only children because we

_____ with other children. Many parents with large families don't have
3. (get married / aren't busy)

_____ time to talk to their children. And, if both parents work, it's very
  4. (enough / siblings)

_____ for them to make time for their kids. Parents of only children don't have
    5. (raise / hard)

this problem.

    We also know that friends are very important to only children. Many of us move to

neighborhoods with lots of young families. It's important to _____ our only
                                    6. (raise / afford)

children in a place where they can make a lot of friends. So, our children are not lonely!

    Here's some interesting information: only 3 percent of American families say that a one-child

family is the best family size. But last month, *Time Magazine* said that one-third (1/3) of young

Americans want to _____ just one child after they _____. Why
            7. (make / have)   **8.** (make money / get married)

is this? Is it because they don't _____ enough _____ at their jobs,
                         9. (make . . . money / have . . . children)

so they _____ to have a bigger family? Maybe. But we think it's also because
    10. (make money / can't afford)

more and more people see that single-child families are wonderful!

Lisa Conner   Jules Conner

Editors, *Only Child Magazine*

---

2   🔘 *Now listen to the audio. Check your answers.*

2 FOCUS ON LISTENING

A LISTENING ONE: Changing Families

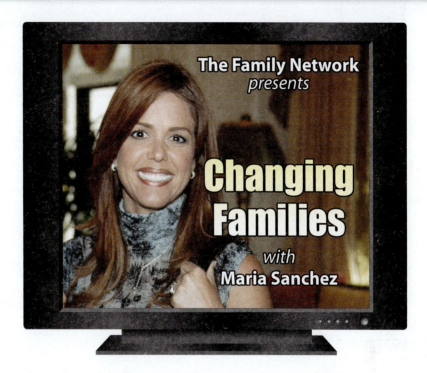

The Family Network
presents

Changing Families

with
Maria Sanchez

Listen to the beginning of Changing Families, *a TV talk show. Then complete the exercises. On the show, the host, Maria Sanchez, talks to two families.*

1. Maria is probably going to ask the parents, "Why did you decide to _____?"
   a. have only one child
   b. become parents

2. What are Maria and the parents going to talk about? Check (✓) your ideas.

   _____ siblings   _____ teachers

   _____ culture   _____ grandparents

   _____ decisions   _____ travel

   _____ money   _____ friends

   _____ age   _____ television

1 CD 2 *Listen to the interview. Complete the sentences with the words and phrases*
   37 *from the box. You will not use all of the words and phrases.*

a good job	a lot of money	hard	problems
a good life	busy	lonely	siblings
a happy child	easy	old	young

1. Today, many people don't believe that only children are

   _____.

2. Marion and Mark think raising a young child is _____.

3. Marion and Mark think Tonia is _____.

4. Tom and Jenna can afford to give one child _____.

5. Jay is usually _____ with his friends, sports, and music.

2 *Now go back to Section 2A, Question 2, on page 173. Were your ideas correct?*

◖ LISTEN FOR DETAILS

CD 2
 38 *Listen again. Write* **T** *(true) or* **F** *(false). Correct the false information.*

_____ **1.** Marion had a baby when she was 36.

_____ **2.** Marion and Mark can't take care of Tonia.

_____ **3.** Tonia spends time with her parents and friends.

_____ **4.** Maria read that many only children are not popular.

_____ **5.** Tom and Jenna made a difficult decision.

_____ **6.** School, music, and traveling are important to Tom and Jenna.

_____ **7.** Sometimes Jay is lonely.

◀ MAKE INFERENCES

Listen to the excerpts from Listening One. Circle the correct answer to complete each sentence.

 **Excerpt One**

1. Marion and Mark ____.
   a. thought about having another child
   b. never thought about having another child

Excerpt Two

2. Mark is probably interested in this information because he thinks ____.
   a. his daughter is more intelligent than other children
   b. other children are more intelligent than his daughter

Excerpt Three

3. Money is ____ important to Tom and Jenna now than in the past.
   a. less
   b. more

◀ EXPRESS OPINIONS

*Read the statements. Mark each one **A** (Agree) or **D** (Disagree). Then discuss your opinions with the class.*

____ **1.** It's better for children to have older parents.

____ **2.** Only children are more popular than children with siblings.

____ **3.** These days, parents need a lot of money to raise children.

B LISTENING TWO: How Do Only Kids Feel?

Now listen to Tonia and Jay, two only children, speaking to Maria Sanchez. Circle the best answer to complete each sentence.

1. Tonia ____ being an only child.
   a. likes
   b. loves
   c. doesn't like

2. Most of Tonia's friends have ____.
   a. siblings
   b. sisters
   c. older parents

Tonia

(continued on next page)

3. Tonia's mother _____ her decision to Tonia.

    a. didn't explain

    b. explained

    c. isn't going to explain

4. How does Tonia feel about her parents' decision? She _____.

    a. understands it and agrees with it

    b. understands it but isn't happy about it

    c. doesn't understand it

5. Jay and Tonia have _____ feelings about being only children.

    a. unusual

    b. the same

    c. different

6. When Jay spends time with his parents, he feels _____.

    a. different

    b. special

    c. uncomfortable

Jay

7. Jay and his parents enjoy _____.

    a. traveling

    b. living in Colorado

    c. staying home

8. Many of Jay's friends don't have _____.

    a. parents

    b. siblings

    c. families

C INTEGRATE LISTENINGS ONE AND TWO

◖ STEP 1: Organize

What are the advantages of having only one child? What are the disadvantages? Think about Listenings One and Two. Write the reasons in the chart. Use the cues in each box for ideas. Then compare your chart with a partner's.

ADVANTAGES	DISADVANTAGES
1. easier / older parents / raise / just It's easier for older parents to raise just one child.	**1.** hard decision / if / love children
2. parents / spend / more / time / child	**2.** some / want / play / children, not adults
3. popular / with siblings	**3.** when parents / busy, / no one / play / at home
4. independent	**4.** lonely
5. some / children / special	**5.** some / different from / friends
6. less expensive / raise / one child	

◀ **STEP 2: Synthesize**

Role-play. Work with a partner. Student A thinks it is good to have more than one child. Student B thinks it is better to have an only child. Complete the conversation with information from Step 1: Organize.

A: Do you really believe that having just one child is best?

B: Of course. It's easier for older parents to raise only one child.

A: But isn't it hard if you love children?

B: Yes, it is. That's true. But parents of an only child can . . .

A: Well, of course, spending time . . .

B: . . .

A: . . .

A VOCABULARY

◖ REVIEW

Work in pairs. Student A, read your sentences aloud. Student B, read your sentences aloud, and fill in the blanks with the correct words from the box.

busy	especially	raise	tired	took care of

A: Did your parents work when you were a child?

B: Yes, but my grandmother lived with us. She helped my parents to

_____ me.
      1.

A: Really? That's so unusual in the U.S.

B: I know, but it was great for me because my parents were always so

_____ with their jobs.
      2.

A: Oh . . .

B: They usually came home late, and then they were really _____.
                                                   3.

A: Sure . . .

B: So my grandmother _____ me during the week.
                                    4.

A: Did you like that?

B: Yeah, it was _____ nice for me because I don't have any
                            5.

siblings.

A: So you weren't lonely because your grandmother was there.

B: Yeah. She always had time to talk and play with me.

A: You were lucky!

B: Yes, I agree!

Now switch roles.

can't afford	hard	make (a lot of) money
got married	have (a baby)	

B: Did I tell you the news about my sister, Joan?

A: Is she going to _____ a baby?
6.

B: Yes, how did you know?

A: Well, she and David _____ two years ago, right?
7.

B: Yeah.

A: And she's 34 or 35 right?

B: Yeah, she's 35.

A: So, that wasn't _____ to guess!
8.

B: OK, I see your point!

A: Is she going to stop working when she has the baby?

B: She really wants to, but she can't. They _____ to live on one
9.

salary.

A: Really? I thought that David had a good job.

B: Well, he likes his job a lot, but he doesn't _____ a lot of
10.

_____ .

1 Read the article from Only Child magazine aloud with a partner. Student A, read all the problems under "This is what THEY say." Then Student B, read all the responses under "Our responses."

Some people think that only children have a lot of problems. Of course, *we* know this is not true!

This is what THEY say:

"Problem" #1:
*Only children are **selfish**.*

Only children get all of their parents' attention. They think they are the most important people in the world. They never think about other people. When children are **selfish**, _____.

"Problem" #2:
*Only children are **spoiled**.*

Parents of only children are sad that their child has no siblings. They think that toys, money, and other things can make their child feel happy. But the child keeps asking for more. When children are **spoiled**, _____.

"Problem" #3:
*Only children **don't get along well with others.***

Only children live with adults, so they don't learn how to play with other children. They feel like "little adults." They feel different from other children, so they don't have good friendships with them. When children **don't get along well with others**, _____.

Our responses:

_____ We and our children are happy with our families. We don't need to buy our children toys to make them happy. But our children spend more time playing by themselves; they learn how to be alone. They are more **independent** than children with siblings. This means _____.

_____ We know that friends are very important for our children. We make sure that our children always have friends to play with. Our children are usually very popular with other children. They **have many close friends**. This means _____.

_____ We give our children the right amount of attention. This makes our children feel good about themselves. They also care about other people. Our children are usually **self-confident**, not self-centered. This means _____.

2 *Match the boldfaced vocabulary in the article with their definitions below. Write the letter of the definition on the line at the end of the paragraph on page 180.*

    a. they have a lot of very good friends

    b. they can do many things without help

    c. they think only about themselves

    d. they believe they are good people, with good abilities

    e. they have problems with other people

    f. they are never satisfied. They always want more and more things

3 *Match the problem in "This is what THEY say" with the best response by* Only Child *magazine. Write the number of the problem on the line before the correct paragraph on page 180.*

4 *Read the article aloud with your partner again. Student A, read one problem. Then Student B, read the correct response.*

◖ CREATE

Work with a small group of students. Talk about each idea in the article. Which ideas do you think are true? Why? Use the vocabulary from Review and Expand.

Example

1. Only children are selfish. / Only children are self-confident.

    STUDENT A: I think only children are selfish. It's natural. Only children spend a lot of time alone. They don't learn how to think about other people's feelings. That's why they are selfish.
    STUDENT B: I'm not sure. I think . . .
    STUDENT C: I . . . because . . .

2. Only children are spoiled. / Only children are independent.

3. Only children don't get along well with others. / Only children have many close friends.

1 *Tonia is talking to Jay after the TV show. Read the conversation. Look at the underlined verbs. Then answer the questions.*

JAY: I'm going to have lunch with my parents. How about you?
TONIA: We are going to visit my grandparents.

1. How many parts does each verb have?

2. What is the first part?

3. What is the second part? Does it change?

4. What's the form of the last part?

THE FUTURE WITH *BE GOING TO*

1. Use *be + going to +* the base form of the verb to talk about an action in the future.	I **am going to have** lunch later. She **is going to visit** her friends tonight.
NOTE: Use contractions in speaking and in informal writing.	**I'm going to have** lunch later. She**'s going to visit** her friends tonight.
2. To make a negative sentence, put *not* before *going to*.	I'm **not going to** travel next week. He's **not going to** have a big family.
NOTE: You can also use the negative contractions *isn't* and *aren't*.	He is**n't going to** get married soon. We are**n't going to** have a big family.
3. To make **yes / no** questions, put a form of *be* **before the subject**.	**Are you** going to visit your grandparents soon? **Is he** going to buy a car next year?
4. To answer **yes / no** questions, you can use a short form: *Yes* + subject + *be* *No* + subject + *be* + *not*	Yes, I am / he is / you are / we are / they are. No, I'm not / he's not / you're not / we're not / they're not.
5. You can use these future time expressions with *be going to*: later, tonight, tomorrow, soon in two days / in a week / in a month / in a year in the future this Tuesday / week / month / year next Monday / week / month / year	**I'm going to** get married **next year**. **We're going to** have dinner together **this week**.

2 Tonia is talking about her plans for the future. Complete the conversation with the correct forms of **be going to**. Then read the conversation aloud with a partner.

MARIA: I know you don't like being an only child. _____ you

_____ have a big family when you grow up?

TONIA: Definitely! I _____ have four or five kids! Maybe six!
2.

MARIA: Well, then your children _____ be lonely!
3.

TONIA: Right. They _____ have a lot of brothers and sisters to
4.

play with.

MARIA: But, you know, raising so many kids is very expensive!

TONIA: Well, I _____ work hard and save a lot of money.
5.

I _____ be rich!
6.

MARIA: What a plan! You're only eight years old and you already know that

you _____ be rich! That's amazing!
7.

3 Work with a small group of students.
   a. On a small piece of paper, write a question using **be going to** and a word or phrase from columns A and B.

   b. Put all of the questions in a paper bag. Give the bag to another group.

   c. Take turns in your group. Select a question from the bag. Read it aloud and answer it using **be going to**.

A	B
go shopping	this year
take a vacation	next week
move to a different city/country	in a month
move to the countryside	soon
see a movie	tonight
visit a good friend	tomorrow
buy a car	in ____ years
have a big family	in the future

Examples

Are you going to move to a different city this year?

Are you going to see a movie tonight?

PRONUNCIATION: "Going to" vs. "Gonna"

We use *be going to* + verb to talk about the future, especially future plans:

I'*m going to take* piano lessons next month.

CD 2
43 Listen to the sentences. How is *going to* pronounced?

A: I'm going to take a vacation next month.
B: I'm going to travel to Europe next week.

PRONOUNCING "GOING TO"

Native speakers pronounce *going to* in two ways:
- In formal or careful (slow) speech, they use the full form:
going to /gówɪŋ tə/
　　　　/gówɪŋ tə/
We're going to spend more money on education.

- In informal or fast speech, native speakers use the reduced form:
gónna /gə́nə/
　　　/gə́nə/
I'm gonna ask my mom if you can come for dinner.

- **NOTE:** We usually do not write *gonna*. *Gonna* is used only in speaking.

- You can use /gówɪŋ tə/ (the careful pronunciation) when you speak.

---

1 **CD 2** *Listen to the sentences. Is **going to** pronounced in the full form or the*
44 *reduced form **(gonna)**? Circle the correct answer. First, listen to the*
examples.

Examples

But my mom said, "_____ have another child."
(a.) I am not going to
b. I'm not gonna

Today, _____ talk about only children.
a. we are going to
(b.) we're gonna

1. Today, _____ meet two families with only children.
   a. we are going to
   b. we're gonna

2. First, _____ talk with Marion and Mark Carter.
   a. we are going to
   b. we're gonna

3. OK, next, _____ talk to the kids!
   a. I am going to
   b. I'm gonna

4. _____ speak to Marion and Mark's daughter, Tonia.
   a. I'm going to
   b. I'm gonna

5. Like, this year, _____ go skiing in Colorado.
   a. we are going to
   b. we're gonna

2 *Match the phrases in column A and column B to make true sentences about you and the people in your family. With a partner, take turns saying your sentences. You can use **going to** or **gonna**. Then share some of your sentences with the class.*

Example

STUDENT 1: "I'm not *going to* have a big family."
STUDENT 2: "I'm *gonna* travel this year."

A	**B**
_____ 1. I'm (not) going to	a. travel this year.
_____ 2. My (wife/husband) is probably (not) going to	b. have just one child.
	c. have a big family.
_____ 3. My (mother/father) is probably (not) going to	d. take a vacation this year.
	e. have a baby soon.
_____ 4. My (brother/sister) is probably (not) going to	f. go skiing next winter.
	g. get married in a few years.
_____ 5. My parents are (not) going to	h. be busy tonight.

◖FUNCTION: Agreeing and Disagreeing

There are many ways to show that you agree or disagree with another person's opinion.

Here are some common phrases you can use.

TO AGREE	TO DISAGREE
I agree (with you). (I think) You're right. (I think) That's true. That's for sure.	I don't agree (with you). I don't think that's true. / I don't think so. That's not true.

WHEN YOU'RE NOT SURE
I'm not sure about that. That may be true. Maybe . . .

Examples
MARION: But . . . well, it's not easy to raise a young child at our age.
MARK: **That's for sure.** We're always tired!
MARIA: I think many young parents feel the same way, too!
MARION: Mmm . . . **Maybe.**

TOM: But, as I'm sure you know, teachers don't make a lot of money!
MARIA: **That's true.** Most teachers aren't rich!

Work with a partner. Student A, read a statement you think is true. Student B, use a phrase to agree, disagree, or say you're not sure about Student A's statement. Then explain why, and state your opinion. Take turns being A and B.

Statements

1. Most only children (*feel / don't feel*) very different from their friends.

2. Only children (*are / are not*) more popular than children with siblings.

3. Many only children (*are / are not*) spoiled.

4. It's (*good / not good*) to be the youngest child in a family.

5. It's (*good / not good*) to be the oldest child in a family.

6. (*All / Not all*) children need siblings.

7. (*Many / Very few*) parents have one child because they're worried that the world has too many people.

8. Only children (*have trouble / don't have trouble*) making friends.

Examples

A: Most only children feel very different from their friends.
B: I don't agree. In most big cities, there are lots of only children!

A: Many only children are not spoiled.
B: That may be true. I think some are, and some aren't.

◖ PRODUCTION: Role-Play

> **In this activity, you will role-play a conversation between Ken and Betsy.** Ken and Betsy are married. They have a four-year-old daughter named Katie. They are talking about having a second child. Ken is 35 years old. He wants to have another child. Betsy is 34. She isn't sure if another child is a good idea. Try to use the vocabulary, grammar, pronunciation, and language for agreeing and disagreeing from the unit.*

Read about Ken, Betsy, and Katie.

Ken	Betsy	Katie
• apartment: nice but very small • rent: expensive		

• job: engineer for a large company
• siblings: two brothers, and they're all very close; thinks it's important to have a sibling
• wants another child?: yes
	• job:
	  –day: teaches singing to private students
	  –night: sings at a jazz club
	• siblings: one brother, but they're not very close; doesn't think it's important to have a sibling
	• wants another child?: not sure
		• she spends time with:
		  –grandmother when Ken and Betsy are working
		  –a lot of friends in the neighborhood
		• she likes to:
		  –read children's books in her room
		  –play with her toys

*For Alternative Speaking Topics, see page 189.

Follow the steps.

Step 1: The teacher will divide the class into two groups.

Step 2: Group A: You are Ken. Make a list of reasons why you want to have another child.

1. It's important for children to have siblings.

2. _____

3. _____

4. _____

5. _____

6. _____

Group B: You are Betsy. Make a list of reasons why you don't want to have another child.

1. Siblings aren't always close.

2. _____

3. _____

4. _____

5. _____

6. _____

Step 3: Work with a partner from the other group. Role-play a conversation between Ken and Betsy. Talk about the future. Use the reasons on your lists. Try to make a decision about having another child.

Step 4: Discuss. Share your decisions with the class. How many pairs decided to have another child? How many decided not to have one?

ALTERNATIVE SPEAKING TOPICS

Discuss one of the topics. Use the vocabulary and grammar from the unit.

1. Look at the graph. What does it show about the number of American families with only one child? Is the same thing happening where you live? Do you know why?

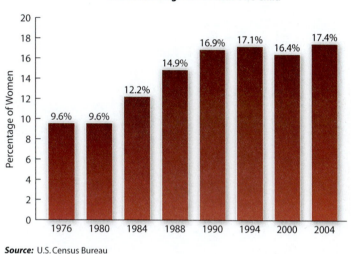

U.S. Women Age 40–44 with One Child

Source: U.S. Census Bureau

2. Do you think it's good to have only one child? Why or why not?

3. How many children do you want to have? (OR: How many children do you have?)

   a. Does your decision have anything to do with the cost of raising a child? (In the U.S, the cost of raising one child for the first 17 years of life is $134,370–$284,460.)

   b. Does your decision have anything to do with the population explosion[1] in the world?

   c. Do you have other reasons? What are they?

RESEARCH TOPICS, see page 221.

RESEARCH TOPICS, see page 221.

---

[1] **population explosion:** the large increase in the number of people in the world

10 The Beautiful Game

Photo 1

Photo 2

1 FOCUS ON THE TOPIC

A PREDICT

Look at the pictures. Discuss the questions with the class.

1. Who are the people in photo 1?
   a. soccer fans   **b.** soccer players

2. Who are the people in photo 2?
   a. soccer fans   **b.** soccer players

3. How do the people in photo 1 feel? What are they doing?

Interview three classmates. Ask the questions and fill in the chart.

	CLASSMATE 1	CLASSMATE 2	CLASSMATE 3
1. What is the national sport in your country?			
2. Do you like to watch this sport?			
3. Do you play this sport?			
4. Is this sport easy to understand?			

C **BACKGROUND** AND **VOCABULARY**

1 CD 2 45 *Work with a partner. Read and listen to a student's presentation about soccer.*

Soccer: The world's most popular sport

Soccer is easy to learn and understand. The only **equipment** you really need is a ball. But a ball can be made of old clothes or almost anything. It's nice to have a good **field** to play on, but you don't even need that—the "field" can also be a street. For the **goal**, you can use two rocks. With a "ball," a "field" to play on, and a few friends, anyone can play.

Soccer is very popular. In most countries, it's called "football." In 2006, 715 million soccer **fans** watched the final World Cup **match** between the French and Italian soccer **teams**. Italy won. The final **score** was 0–1.

People of all **nationalities** love soccer. When a player makes a point, people all over the world say "Goal!" *Goal* is almost a **universal** word.

Everyone loves soccer!

Here are the names of some other countries where people play soccer. Next to them are the nationalities that describe the people from these countries.

Country	Nationality	Country	Nationality
Argentina	Argentinian/Argentinean/Argentine	Italy	Italian
Australia	Australian	Japan	Japanese
Brazil	Brazilian	Kenya	Kenyan
Canada	Canadian	Korea	Korean
Chile	Chilean	Mexico	Mexican
China	Chinese	Netherlands	Dutch
Croatia	Croatian	Norway	Norwegian
Czech Republic	Czech	Portugal	Portuguese
Ecuador	Ecuadorian/Ecuadorean	Senegal	Senegalese
France	French	Spain	Spanish
Germany	German	Turkey	Turkish
Iraq	Iraqi	United Kingdom	British
Israel	Israeli	United States	American

2 *Choose the correct definition to complete each sentence.*

1. Equipment is the (*things / money*) you need to play a sport or finish a project.

2. Fans are people who like to (*play / watch*) a sport.

3. A field is a place where you (*play sports / buy equipment*).

4. A goal is the place where soccer players (*get practice / get points*).

5. A match is a (*game / ball*).

6. Your nationality is the country that you (*are from / visit*).

7. A score is (*the numbers that show who is winning a game / the people who play a sport together*).

8. Teams are groups of people who (*watch / play*) sports together.

9. If something is universal, (*everyone in the world can understand it / it is not from your country*).

2 FOCUS ON LISTENING

A LISTENING ONE: The Sports File

1 CD 2 46 *Listen to the beginning of the short radio show called* The Sports File. *Today's show is about soccer.*

2 *What do you think you will hear on the show? Check (✓) the items.*

_____ voices of people who love soccer

_____ Americans talking about baseball

_____ why soccer is so popular

_____ how to become a professional soccer player

LISTEN FOR MAIN IDEAS

CD 2 47 *Listen to the radio show. Circle the correct answer.*

1. The main question that Jane Tuttle wants to answer is _____.
    a. Do Americans love soccer?
    b. Why are so many people watching soccer at Paolinho's?
    c. Why do people from most countries love soccer?

2. The three people she talked to are all _____.
    a. soccer fans from around the world
    b. sports fans from the U.S.
    c. soccer players on U.S. teams

LISTEN FOR DETAILS

1 CD 2 48 *Listen again. Check (✓) two correct details about each person on* The Sports File.

1. Gilberto

    _____ **a.** is Brazilian.

    _____ **b.** doesn't understand Jane's question.

    _____ **c.** thinks soccer is a beautiful part of life.

    _____ **d.** thinks soccer matches need music.

2. Jose

_____ **a.** is Mexican.

_____ **b.** thinks most soccer players speak English.

_____ **c.** thinks soccer brings people together.

_____ **d.** thinks there are two countries in the world.

3. Anders

_____ **a.** is Norwegian.

_____ **b.** thinks people in the U.S. don't understand soccer.

_____ **c.** thinks American football is hard to understand.

_____ **d.** says you need to play well to learn soccer.

4. Jane

_____ **a.** is a reporter for _The Sports File._

_____ **b.** talked to Gilberto, Jose, and Anders by phone.

_____ **c.** says that she dislikes soccer.

_____ **d.** wants to help people in the U.S. understand soccer.

2 _Now go back to Section 2A, Question 2, on page 194. Were your ideas correct?_

◖ MAKE INFERENCES

Listen to the excerpts from Listening One. Choose the best answer to each question. Then discuss your answer with a partner.

 **Excerpt One**

1. Why does Jane go to a pizza restaurant to learn about soccer?
   a. She is hungry for pizza.
   b. Soccer fans will be there to watch the World Cup.
   c. Soccer players like to go there after their games.

Excerpt Two

2. Why does Jose say that there are only two countries?
   a. People play soccer in only two countries.
   b. Soccer is big in all countries except the United States.
   c. Only one country loves soccer.

(continued on next page)

Excerpt Three

3. How can people learn about soccer at Paolinho's?

  a. They can meet soccer fans.
  b. They can watch soccer on a big TV.
  c. They can play soccer.

◀ **EXPRESS OPINIONS**

1 *On a scale of 1 to 6, where 1 means "not at all" and 6 means "a lot," how much do you like soccer? Put an X where your opinion is.*

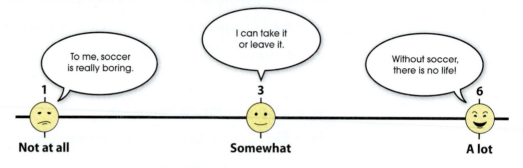

1	3	6
Not at all	Somewhat	A lot

To me, soccer is really boring.

I can take it or leave it.

Without soccer, there is no life!

2 *Write reasons for your opinion.*

  1. _____

  2. _____

3 *In groups of three or four, compare and discuss your opinions.*

B **LISTENING TWO: America Talks**

America Talks is a radio call-in show in the U.S. Listeners call the show and give their opinions.

*Listen to America Talks. Write **T** (true) or **F** (false). Correct the false information.*

_____ **1.** People call *America Talks* from all over the world.

_____ **2.** Bob thinks Americans prefer games with high scores.

_____ **3.** Steve thinks sports fans in the U.S. need a new sport.

_____ **4.** Drew says Pele didn't play soccer in the U.S.

_____ **5.** Drew thinks that the U.S. needs a soccer star.

STEP 1: Organize

Write the number of each sentence in the correct column. Use the information from Listenings One and Two.

1. People from all countries can understand the rules of soccer.

2. Soccer is an art.

3. Adults in the U.S. never learned to play soccer well.

4. People can play it without a lot of expensive equipment.

5. Soccer doesn't have high scores.

6. Soccer sometimes ends in a tie.

7. There are no soccer stars from the U.S.

8. Soccer brings people from many nations together.

9. People in the U.S. did not grow up watching soccer on TV or listening to it on the radio.

WHY SOCCER IS POPULAR IN MOST COUNTRIES	WHY SOCCER IS NOT POPULAR IN THE U.S.
_____	_____
_____	_____
_____	_____
_____	_____
_____	_____
_____	_____
_____	_____
_____	_____

Role-play with a partner. Student A is an international student, and Student B is from the U.S. Student A, explain to Student B why soccer is a great game. Student B, explain why Americans don't like soccer. Use the information from Step 1: Organize. Begin like this:

A: I heard that most Americans don't like soccer. Is that true?
B: Yes, it is.
A: Why? Soccer is so easy to understand.
B: One reason is that . . .
A: . . .
B: . . .

③ FOCUS ON SPEAKING

A VOCABULARY

◀ **REVIEW**

Cross out the word or phrase in parentheses that does not make sense.

1. Do you have the right <u>equipment</u> to go skiing? You'll need (*skis / boots / a car*).

2. The Real Madrid soccer <u>fans</u> were shouting ("*Reee—aaaal!*" / "*Goooal!*" / "*Ball*").

3. No one is in front of the <u>goal</u>! You can (*take it / kick the ball in / make a point*).

4. Let's leave when this (*study / tennis / soccer*) <u>match</u> is over.

5. What is your <u>nationality</u>? I am (*Algerian / French / Parisian*).

6. The <u>score</u> was (*14 to 2 / 3 nothing / almost finished*).

7. Look at the <u>teams</u>. (*They look tired. / He is angry. / They played well.*)

8. Don doesn't like <u>ties</u> because (*nobody wins / you don't know who is best / you can't watch those games*).

9. It's important to follow the <u>rules</u> in (*television / soccer / school*).

10. Basketball is <u>universal</u>. People play it in (*Croatia, Norway, and Senegal / Chile, Kenya, and New Zealand / New York, Chicago, and Detroit*).

1 *Read the conversation with a partner. The boldfaced expressions are idioms related to sports.*

JOSE: So, Doug, what's going on over there?

DOUG: Oh, that's where Calvin is working.

JOSE: Isn't he a good worker?

DOUG: He was, but he completely **dropped the ball**. Look. He's not even here today.

JOSE: What about the other workers? Why aren't they working over there?

DOUG: That's Calvin's part of the project. They never work with him. Calvin is not a **team player**.

JOSE: It looks like it's hard to **keep the ball rolling** if you have Calvin on your job.

DOUG: It is. I spoke with Mr. Tower about the problem. I wanted Calvin to move to another job so I could get someone better. But Mr. Tower said he didn't want to make any changes.

JOSE: Well, Mr. Tower **calls the shots** . . .

DOUG: He sure does. He told me I just had to **keep my eye on the ball** and get the job done.

2 *Write the correct boldfaced expression from the conversation in each sentence.*

1. A _____ works well with other people.

2. Someone who _____ makes the decisions.

3. If you _____ you continue doing something right.

4. To _____ means to pay attention.

5. If someone _____, he or she didn't finish something.

◀ CREATE

1 *Work in small groups. Have a conversation by answering the following questions. Use the vocabulary from Review and Expand.*

What is a sport?

Are cheerleading, poker, and eating contests sports?

Example

A: I think a sport is a game with a ball and a goal.

B: I disagree. There are some sports, such as tennis and cheerleading, that don't have a goal.

C: Is cheerleading a sport? You don't use a ball in cheerleading . . .

2 *Practice your conversation. Then share it with the class.*

B GRAMMAR: *Should* for Ideas and Opinions

1 *Read the sentences. Underline the main verbs in each sentence. Circle the word that comes before each verb.*

You shouldn't stay home.

You should join us at Paolinho's for the next game.

Sports should be easy to understand.

Games should not have a lot of rules.

SHOULD FOR IDEAS AND OPINIONS

1. Use *should* to tell someone that you think it is **a good idea** to do something.	You **should** do your homework every night.
2. You can also use *should* to give your opinion about **something**.	School **should** be fun.
3. Use *should* + **base form of the verb.**	[should + simple form of verb] You **should come** home early. [should + simple form of verb] He **should be** a team player.
4. Use *should not* (or *shouldn't*) **+ base form of the verb in the negative.**	[shouldn't + simple form of verb] You **shouldn't stay** out late. [shouldn't + simple form of verb] Soccer **shouldn't be** difficult to learn.
5. For questions, use **question word + should + subject + base form of the verb.**	**When should we go** to Paolino's? **Should we go** now?

2 *Sarah wants to learn to play soccer. Fill in the blanks with* **should** *or* **shouldn't**.

1. She _____ learn to kick the ball into the goal.

2. She _____ find some friends to play with.

3. She and her friends _____ watch soccer on TV.

4. Sarah _____ bring her baseball bat to the games.

5. She _____ wear good shoes to practice.

6. She _____ run with the ball in her hands.

3 *Anders is giving more opinions about what he thinks a good sport is. Use the words to make sentences with* **should**.

1. Good sports / not have / lots of rules

_____

2. Players / make / a lot of money

_____

(continued on next page)

3. TV sports / not have / advertisements

_____

4. Players / be / strong

_____

4 _Write your own opinions, using_ **should** _and_ **shouldn't**.

1. Sports should _____

2. Sports shouldn't _____

3. Players should _____

4. Players shouldn't _____

C SPEAKING

◀ **PRONUNCIATION: Stress on Important Words**

In many sentences, one word has more important information than the others. The most important word often gives new information. Sometimes it corrects a mistake in the sentence before it. In English, these important words are stressed. They are longer and louder than the other words. They are also pronounced on a higher note.

CD 2
53 _Listen to how the important words sound._

DAD: Maya, get your **soc**cer shoes.

MAYA: I've **got** them. But I can't find my **wa**ter bottle.

1 CD 2
54 _Listen to the conversations. Listen again and repeat each line. Then practice with a partner._

1. **A:** Sammy made a GOAL.
   B: He made THREE goals.

2. **A:** I'm TIRED of baseball.
   B: You should watch the SOCCER match today.

3. **A:** I WATCH soccer, but I don't PLAY it.
   B: You should TRY it. It's FUN.

4. **A:** The Japanese team is very GOOD.
   B: Yeah. They won the ASIA Cup a few years ago.

5. **A:** Soccer's very POPular here.
   B: Yeah. Everyone PLAYS it or WATCHES it.

6. **A:** What kind of SHOES are you looking for?
   B: BASketball shoes.

2 *Work with a partner. Read the sentences together. Decide which word should be stressed (louder and longer) the most. Now, take turns. Read sentence a or b aloud. Do not read the explanation in parentheses. Your partner will tell you if you are saying* **a** *or* **b**.

1. **a.** I don't really like watching sports on TV. (But I like watching other programs.)
   b. I don't really like watching sports on TV. (But I like watching sports live.)

2. **a.** All kids should learn to play sports. (not just a few kids)
   b. All kids should learn to play sports. (But they usually don't.)

3. **a.** Zizou got kicked out of[1] the World Cup final. (That's the most important game of all!)
   b. Zizou got kicked out of the World Cup final. (Oh no! He was one of France's best players!)

4. **a.** Players usually play for their home countries in the World Cup. (but not for other competitions)
   b. Players usually play for their home countries in the World Cup. (not on another country's team)

3 *Look at the list of games on the right.*
   a. *Can you add the names of any other games or activities? Write them in the blanks.*

Questions	Games
Do you like to play GAMES?	Board games: chess, Monopoly, _____
What games do you LIKE?	Puzzles: Sudoku, crossword puzzles, _____
What games are popular IN YOUR COUNTRY?	Electronic games: video games, computer games, _____
	Card games: poker, _____
	Other: karaoke, _____

   b. *Work in small groups. Take turns asking questions. Find out what kinds of activities the people in your group like to play. When you answer a question, make the important information long and loud.*

---

[1]**get kicked out of:** to be told to leave

◀ FUNCTION: Introducing Reasons and Results

There are many ways to introduce reasons in English. The most common one is *because*. There are also many ways to introduce results. Two are *so* and *that's why*.

[result]   [reason]
I love soccer **because** it's exciting.

      [reason]   [result]
Soccer is exciting, **so** I love it.

      [reason]   [result]
Soccer is exciting. **That's why** I love it.

*Nicole found a list of Winter Olympic sports in the newspaper. She made notes about what she wants to watch and what she doesn't want to watch. Look at the list. With a partner, discuss what she is and isn't going to watch. Explain her reasons. Use **because**, **so**, and **that's why**.*

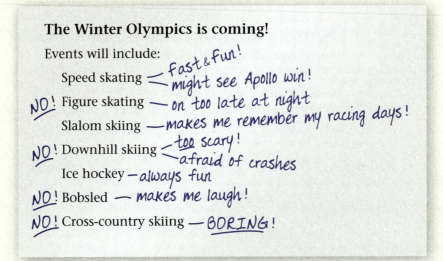

The Winter Olympics is coming!

Events will include:

Speed skating — *fast & fun!*
might see Apollo win!
NO! Figure skating — *on too late at night*
Slalom skiing — *makes me remember my racing days!*
NO! Downhill skiing — *too scary!*
afraid of crashes
Ice hockey — *always fun*
NO! Bobsled — *makes me laugh!*
NO! Cross-country skiing — *BORING!*

Examples

Nicole isn't going to watch cross-country skiing because she thinks it's boring.

Speed skating is fast and fun, so Nicole is going to watch it.

Speed skating is fast and fun. That's why Nicole is going to watch it.

Nicole might see Apollo win. That's why she's going to watch speed skating.

Famous people sell sports. Basketball was not very popular in the U.S. until Michael Jordan became famous and made it popular. Many people watch football or baseball to see their favorite players. ***In this activity, you will make a 30-second TV ad for a soccer game that will be on TV next week in the U.S.*** You are a famous soccer player, and you want to convince Americans to watch this game. Try to use the vocabulary, grammar, pronunciation, and language for introducing reasons and results from the unit.*

Step 1: Make notes for your performance.

   a. Decide on your message. What is your main point? TV ads are very short, so you need to give a clear message in a short time. (For example, "The whole world is watching soccer. You should watch it, too!")

   b. Write the main message in one sentence. Choose your words carefully. Think about how stressed words can help you give your message.

   c. Look back over the unit and choose one or two reasons to support your message. You can also use reasons that are not in the unit.

   d. Make notes about the reason(s) that you want to include, but do not write out all of the exact words that you will say.

Step 2: Practice with a partner. As you listen to each other, answer the questions.

   a. Is the message clear?

   b. What are the reasons for someone to watch the game on TV?

   c. Do the stressed words help to make the message clear?

   d. Will the ad convince people to watch the soccer game?

Step 3: Discuss one or two ways to improve the presentation.

Step 4: Perform your ad for the class (or record it on video).

---

*For Alternative Speaking Topics, see page 206.

Step 5:

a. As you watch your classmates' ads, answer the question below on a piece of paper. Give this information to the presenter at the end of class.

Name of presenter: _____

What was the main message? _____

b. Vote on the best ad.

c. Read your classmates' notes to you. Was your message clear? How could you make it better?

ALTERNATIVE SPEAKING TOPICS

Discuss one of the topics. Use the vocabulary and grammar from the unit.

1. Discuss the reasons that you like (or dislike) soccer. Are these reasons similar to the reasons in the unit?

2. Many people say that basketball and soccer are similar games. Do you think they are similar? Compare these two games.

3. Are baseball, basketball, and American football popular where you grew up? Why or why not? Did you play one of these sports?

RESEARCH TOPICS, see page 222.

STUDENT ACTIVITIES

UNIT 2: Recycled Fashion

Present Progressive, Page 36

5 *Student B, listen to Student A. Answer Student A's questions about your picture. Then, ask Student A **yes / no** questions about his or her picture. Try to find three or four differences between the pictures. Use the present progressive.*

Example

B: Do you have a picture of a man?
A: No, a woman.
B: Is she buying something?
A: No, she isn't.
B: Is she ____ing . . . ?
A: . . .

◀ **REVIEW, Page 53**

Student B, listen to Student A. Then, continue the conversation, choosing the sentences that make sense. If you think that your partner chose the wrong sentence, say "I don't think that makes sense."

Conversation 1: "I don't like rap."

No, I think rappers are real musicians.

2. OR

No, I don't think rap is really music.

You're right. They don't sing or play any musical instruments.

4. OR

You're right. They play a lot of musical instruments.

And the words are so bad! I don't understand why rap is so popular.

6. OR

And the words are so bad! That's why rap isn't popular.

I guess different people like different types of music.

8. OR

I guess everyone likes the same types of music.

Student B, read sentence 1. Then, continue the conversation, choosing the sentences that make sense.

Conversation 2: "Do you like Brazilian jazz?"

1. Did you ever hear Brazilian jazz?

   I know! I just bought an old CD by Tom Jobim.
3. OR

   I know! I just bought an old CD by a famous rapper.

   He's 80, I think.
5. OR

   In the 80s, I think.

   At a great music store in my neighborhood.
7. OR

   I live in a great neighborhood!

◀ **PRONUNCIATION, Page 78**

4 *Work with a partner to complete the times that are missing in your schedule. Ask your partner for the missing information. Use the verbs in your chart to tell Student A the information he / she is missing. Do the example:*

Example

A: Do you know about ___the bus from New York to Kingston?___

B: ___Yes, it leaves at 2 P.M. and arrives at 3:45 P.M.___

STUDENT A'S SCHEDULE	TIMES	
The bus from New York to Kingston	_____	_____

STUDENT B'S SCHEDULE	TIMES	
The bus from New York to Kingston (leave, arrive)	2 P.M.	3:45 P.M.

STUDENT B'S SCHEDULE	TIMES	
The Hope Diamond tour	_____	_____
The museum	_____	_____
The movie *Blood Diamond* (verbs: start, end)	8:00 P.M.	10:10 P.M.
The train from New York to Montreal, Canada (verbs: leave, arrive)	8:15 A.M.	6:30 P.M.

❨ REVIEW, Page 92

Listen to Student A. Choose the correct response.

- That's great. But your family may need some **support**, too.

- I'm sorry to hear that. It's a terrible illness.

- Maybe she can **join** a **support** group. Then she can make some new friends.

- Yes, people with Alzheimer's often **forget** names, even the names of their **family members**.

Switch roles. Read each sentence. Listen to your partner's response. Does it make sense? If it doesn't make sense, tell your partner, "I don't think that's right."

5. When Elsa got Alzheimer's **disease**, she couldn't keep her job as a nurse.

6. Elsa can't **remember** things that happened yesterday or last week.

7. Elsa joined a **support group**, and she made friends with the other **members**.

8. A psychologist helps the **members** of **Elsa's** support group.

Respond to Student A's sentences. Where you see a blank, interrupt Student A with a phrase from the box. Switch roles in Conversation 2.

Sorry, (but)	Excuse me,
I'm sorry, (but)	(I'm) sorry for interrupting, but . . .

Conversation 1

2. Really? Do you meditate?

4. _____ did you say you meditate for twenty minutes every day?

6. _____ how does it help you?

8. _____ do you mean you meditate on your own *and* with a group?

10. That sounds great.

Now you begin the conversation. Read the sentences. Student A will interrupt you in sentences 3, 5, and 7.

Conversation 2

1. I have some good news. I stopped smoking!

3. I joined *Smokenders.* I go to their meetings every . . .

5. Oh, it's a support group. They help people who want to stop smoking . . .

7. Well, I learned that I smoked a lot when I was nervous. So they taught me to relax . . .

9. No. When I need to relax, I exercise. Now I never want to smoke!

◀ **REVIEW, Page 133**

Listen to Student A. Complete your responses with a word or phrase from the box. Switch roles after sentence 4.

beat (someone) up	destroy	jail	violence
democracy	encouraged	political	without

1b. That's right. Wangari _____ the women to continue working for a new government.

2b. That's true, but he couldn't _____ the group.

3b. Yes, they _____ her _____. She had to go to the hospital.

4b. Yes, he put other members of the Green Belt Organization in _____, too.

Now read each sentence below aloud. Listen to Student A's response. If it doesn't make sense, tell your partner, "I don't think that's right."

5a. Rigoberta believed that people <u>did not need</u> a war to change the government.

6a. Rigoberta told the Guatemalan people not to <u>fight</u>.

7a. Rigoberta wanted <u>the Guatemalan people to choose their own government</u>.

8a. Rigoberta Menchu won the Nobel Peace Prize because she worked hard to change her country's <u>government</u>.

RESEARCH TOPICS

UNIT 1: Faraway Friends

◀ RESEARCH

The Friendship Force works for world peace. Learn about another organization that works for world peace.

Step 1: Choose an organization. You may choose from the list below.

Step 2: Get information about the organization. Use the Internet or a library.

Step 3: Give a report about the organization to a small group of your classmates.

- United States Peace Corps
- Médecins sans Frontières (Doctors without Borders)
- Seeds of Peace
- World Peace Project for Children
- Artists without Borders
- Kids without Borders
- Peace through the Arts Camp

Questions to Guide Your Research

1. What is the name of the organization?
2. Who can belong to the organization?
3. What do they do?
4. Where did the organization begin? When?
5. Are you interested in this organization? Why or why not?

◀ LISTENING ACTIVITY

Listen to your classmates' reports. Write the name of the organization, and ask two questions to get more information.

UNIT 2: Recycled Fashion

◀ RESEARCH

Find a person outside of class. Interview this person about fashion using the questions below. Take notes. Then share your report with the class.

1. On a scale of 1 to 10, how important is fashion to you?

1	5	10
not important	somewhat important	very important

2. Do you like vintage clothing? Do you wear vintage clothing?

3. What do you think about using old materials to make new clothes?

4. How often do you wear traditional clothing? Do you enjoy wearing it?

◀ LISTENING ACTIVITY

Listen to your classmates' reports. Ask for more information.

UNIT 3: Rap Music

◀ RESEARCH

Step 1: Choose a song that you like very much. Get some information about it on the Internet. You can use the singer's name, the songwriter's name, the name of the song, and the word "lyrics" as key words for your Internet search. Then use your information to complete the sentences.

(My friends and) I usually listen to _____ music.
(kind of music)

I like to listen to music on _____.
(**CDs**, my iPod, etc.)

Today I'm going to **play** one of **my favorite** songs. The name of

this song is _____. It's on the CD / album

_____.
(name of the CD / album)

The (singer's / band's / group's) name is _____.

I _____ The songwriter's name is
(how much **do I like** this singer / band)

_____. This song is _____
(what kind of music)

music. It is about _____. This song came out in
(story or idea of the song)

_____. This song (is **popular** now / was **popular**)
(year)

_____.
(when)

The words in this song _____. I think this
(are important, **rhyme**, are **slang**, etc.)

is a (**great**) song because (I like) the _____.
(words, melody, etc.)

When I listen to this song, I (**feel / think about / remember**) _____.
(what)

That's why **I like** this song.

Do you have any questions?

Step 2: Bring the CD or tape to class. Write the name of the song and the singer / band on the blackboard.

Step 3: Play a short part of the song for the class or a small group of classmates. Tell them about the song and singers, but DON'T READ from your book or paper.

◖ LISTENING ACTIVITY

Listen to your classmates' presentations. Ask questions about each song.

May I ask (you) a question?

Can I ask (you) a question?

You may also need to ask:

Could you make it louder, please? OR Could you turn it up, please?

Could you make it softer, please? OR Could you turn it down, please?

⟨ RESEARCH

Complete one of the research activities.

1. Go to a public place such as a park or a shopping center. Look at the different types of jewelry and possessions that people have.

Place: _____

I. What kind of jewelry do you see (for example, rings, necklaces, bracelets, earrings)?

2. Who is wearing the most jewelry—children, teenagers, young adults, middle-aged adults, or older adults?

3. What other valuable possessions do you see (for example, purses, cell phones, cameras)?

---

2. Talk to people you know. Ask at least one man, one woman, one young adult, and one teenager why a piece of jewelry that they are wearing is valuable. Write it in the chart.

PERSON	MEANING
Adult man	His wife gave him the ring. It's his wedding ring.
Adult woman	
Young adult	
Teenager	

In class, form groups with students who did the same research. Compare your answers. Tell the class the most interesting information your group found.

⟨ LISTENING ACTIVITY

Listen to your classmates. What kind of jewelry is valuable to men? To women? To young adults? To teenagers? What other valuable things do many people have?

◀ RESEARCH

Interview an elderly or middle-aged person that you know (a family member, friend, neighbor, or teacher), using the questions below. Begin like this:

May I ask you some questions about your life?

Do you mind if I ask you some questions about your life?

Interview Questions

About the past:

1. What is your earliest memory?
2. Where did you grow up?
3. Where did you go to school?
4. Did you have a best friend in school? What did you like about this person?
5. What was your first job? Did you like it?
6. What is your happiest memory?

About now:

7. Do you work? What do you (OR did you) do?
8. Do you have any hobbies?
9. Who is your best friend now?
10. Are you a member of any groups? What kind?
11. Your questions: _____

Tell the class one interesting thing about the person you interviewed.

◀ LISTENING ACTIVITY

Listen to your classmates' reports. While your classmates are speaking, take turns interrupting politely to ask a question.

UNIT 6: Thinking Young: Creativity in Business

◖RESEARCH

Complete one of the research activities.

1. Find out about a young business owner or entrepreneur (18 years old or younger). Look in the library, in business magazines, or on the Internet, or tell about a person you know. If you use the Internet, look up the key words "young entrepreneurs." Share your information with the class.

2. Watch the movie *Big,* starring Tom Hanks. In this film, 13-year-old Josh wants to be big, like an adult. His wish comes true. His body grows big, but his mind stays young. He gets a job at a toy company. Discuss the film and its connection with this unit. Use the vocabulary from the unit.

job **perks**	**to come up with** a new idea
the **features** of an office	**to save time**
to get around	**to make someone feel** + *adjective* (happy,
to **increase creativity**	relaxed, etc.)
	to be / feel stressed out

◖LISTENING ACTIVITY

Listen to your classmates' reports. Ask questions.

UNIT 7: Planting Trees for Peace

◖RESEARCH

Choose a famous woman. Find out about her. Get information from the library, from the Internet, or from people you know. Here are some ideas:

- Oprah Winfrey (U.S.)
- Eva Peron (Argentina)
- J. K. Rowling (England)
- Hanae Mori (Japan)
- Princess Diana (England)
- Mother Teresa (India)

Use these questions to help with your research. Take notes.

1. When was she born?

2. What is / was her job?

3. What do you know about her work?

4. What do you know about her personal life?

5. In your opinion, why is she important?

6. Your questions:

_____

_____

Give a short report to the class.

◖ LISTENING ACTIVITY

Listen to your classmates' reports. Ask questions. Think about the women your classmates talked about. Which woman was the most important? Why?

UNIT 8: Driving You Crazy

◖ RESEARCH

Find a person outside the class. Interview this person about driving. Use the questions below. Take notes. Share your report with the class.

1. Do you drive? If so, how do you usually drive (carefully, slowly, fast)?

2. Do you ever feel road rage or parking rage?

3. Do you ever see examples of road rage?

4. Why is road rage more common today than a few years ago?

5. Are you afraid of anything when you drive, or when you are a passenger in a car?

6. Your question: _____

◖ LISTENING ACTIVITY

Listen to your classmates' reports. Ask for more information.

◖ RESEARCH

Step 1: Interview a friend, neighbor, or teacher. Ask the questions below. Take notes. You can begin like this:

May I ask you some questions about your family?

Do you mind if I ask you some questions about your family?

Question: Do you have any brothers or sisters?

If the answer is *no,* ask . . .

1. Did you like being an only child when you were younger? Do you like it now? Why or why not?

2. What's the best thing about being an only child? What's the worst thing?

3. Did you ever feel lonely as a child, or did you learn to do things on your own? What did you do when you were alone?

4. Who did you play with?

5. Why did your parents decide to have only one child? Do you know their reason?

6. Did you get a lot of attention from your parents?

7. Your question:

   _____

If the answer is *yes,* ask . . .

1. How many siblings do you have? (How many brothers and how many sisters?)

2. Are you the oldest, the youngest, or a middle child?

3. When you were a child, did you like being the (oldest / youngest / middle) child? Why or why not?

4. What was the best thing about being the (oldest / youngest / middle) child? What was the worst thing about it?

5. Did you get along well with your siblings when you were children? How about now?

6. Did you get enough attention from your parents?

7. Your question:

   _____

Step 2: Work in groups of three. Give a short report about the person you interviewed.

◖ LISTENING ACTIVITY

Listen to your classmates' reports. Ask questions.

◖ RESEARCH

Do a survey. Find out what sports are most popular in your city or at your school.

Step 1: In your group, decide on the questions you will ask people. It is important to ask the same questions as the other people in the group.

Possible Questions:

1. Which sport do you like to watch the most on TV—baseball, football, basketball, or soccer (you can add more sports or change these sports if you want)? Why?

2. Which sports are most fun to play?

Step 2: With your group, decide where to go to ask people questions.

Step 3: Do the survey. Each person should talk to at least five people. Take notes on your conversations.

You can begin your conversation like this:

Excuse me, I am doing a survey about sports. Do you have one minute to answer a couple of questions?

Step 4: Bring the information back to your group. Add up the numbers.

Step 5: Give a short presentation to your class.

◖ LISTENING ACTIVITY

Listen to your classmates' reports. Ask for more information.

GRAMMAR BOOK REFERENCES

NorthStar: Listening and Speaking Level 1, Second Edition	Focus on Grammar Level 1, Second Edition	Azar's Basic English Grammar, Third Edition
Unit 1 Present and Past Tense of *Be*	**Part II** The Verb *Be*: Present **Part III** The Verb *Be*: Past	**Chapter 1** Using *Be* **Chapter 3** Using the Simple Present **Chapter 8** Expressing Past Time, Part 1
Unit 2 Present Progressive	**Part V** The Present Progressive	**Chapter 4** Using the Present Progressive
Unit 3 Simple Present Tense with Non-Action (Stative) Verbs	**Part IV** The Simple Present **Unit 14** The Present Progressive: Statements	**Chapter 3** Using the Simple Present **Chapter 5** Talking About the Present
Unit 4 The Simple Present	**Part IV** The Simple Present	**Chapter 3** Using the Simple Present
Unit 5 *Like to, Want to, Need to*		**Chapter 5** *Need* and *Want* + a Noun or an Infinitive: 5-9 *Would Like* vs. *Like*: 5-11
Unit 6 *There is / There are, There was / There were*	**Unit 26** *There is / There are*	**Chapter 5** *There + Be*: 5-4 *There + Be*: Yes / No Questions: 5-5

(continued on next page)

NorthStar: Listening and Speaking Level 1, Second Edition	Focus on Grammar Level 1, Second Edition	Azar's Basic English Grammar, Third Edition
Unit 7 Simple Past Tense	**Part VII** The Simple Past	**Chapter 8** Expressing Past Time, Part 1 **Chapter 9** Expressing Past Time, Part 2
Unit 8 Simple Past and Past Progressive	**Part V** The Present Progressive **Part VII** The Simple Past	**Chapter 9** The Present Progressive and the Past Progressive: 9-9 Simple Past vs. Past Progressive: 9-12
Unit 9 The Future with *Be Going To*	**Part X** The Future with *Be Going To*	**Chapter 10** Future Time: Using *Be Going To*: 10-1
Unit 10 *Should* for Ideas and Opinions		**Chapter 13** Using *Should*: 13-1 Modal Auxiliaries: 13-7

AUDIOSCRIPT

UNIT 1: Faraway Friends

2A. LISTENING ONE: *Hello. This is the Friendship Force.*

Recording: Hello. This is the Friendship Force. The Friendship Force helps people make friends all over the world. We think "A world of friends is a world of peace." For more information about the Friendship Force, press 1. To speak with someone about Friendship Force international groups, press 2.

Rick: Hello, Friendship Force. Rick speaking.

Nina: Hi, umm . . . my name is Nina Rodriguez, and I'm interested in the Friendship Force.

Rick: Good!

Nina: But, um, I have some questions.

Rick: Sure, what do you want to know, Nina?

LISTEN FOR MAIN IDEAS

Recording: Hello. This is the Friendship Force. The Friendship Force helps people make friends all over the world. We think "A world of friends is a world of peace." For more information about the Friendship Force, press 1. To speak with someone about Friendship Force international groups, press 2.

Rick: Hello, Friendship Force. Rick speaking.

Nina: Hi, umm . . . my name is Nina Rodriguez, and I'm interested in the Friendship Force.

Rick: Great!

Nina: But, um, I have some questions.

Rick: Sure, what do you want to know, Nina?

Nina: Well, first, can college students be in the Friendship Force?

Rick: Sure. We have people of all ages—teenagers, college students, even grandparents!

Nina: Oh, that's great. And, how many people travel together?

Rick: Mmmm . . . usually between 15 and 30. Each group is from the same city. So everyone can make friends before they go to the new country.

Nina: That's a good idea.

Rick: Uh-huh. But you don't all stay together in the new country. Each person stays with a different host family, you know, in their home.

Nina: Yeah, I understand that.

Rick: OK, good. Because Friendship Force visitors never stay in hotels.

Nina: Oh, that isn't a problem for me. I think living with a family is the best way to learn about a country.

Rick: OK, then. So, what country do you want to go to?

Nina: Well, I'm really interested in Thailand.

Rick: Thailand is a beautiful country.

Nina: But what about the language? I only speak English.

Rick: Oh, that isn't a problem. Some host families speak English or other languages. But Friendship Force visitors and host families always become good friends.

Nina: Really? Even if they don't speak the same language?

Rick: Language isn't so important! They always understand each other. You'll see!

Nina: OK, that's good. Umm . . . I just have one more question.

Rick: OK.

Nina: Do the visitors have any time to travel?

Rick: Yes, they do. Most visitors spend one or two weeks with their host family first. Then, after that, they travel around the country. But you know, at the Friendship Force, we say, "People, not places" . . .

Nina: Oh . . .

Rick: . . . because we think making new friends is the most important thing.

Nina: I think so, too!

Rick: Good. Any more questions?

Nina: No, I think that's it. Oh—where can I get an application?

Rick: There's an application on our website.

Nina: OK, great. I'm really excited about the Friendship Force! Thank you so much for your help.

Rick: You're welcome, Nina. And good luck.

Nina: Thanks.

Rick: OK, bye now. Take care.

Nina: Bye.

LISTEN FOR DETAILS

(Listen again to Listen for Main Ideas.)

MAKE INFERENCES

Excerpt One

Rick: . . . what do you want to know, Nina?

Nina: Well, first, can college students be in the Friendship Force?

Rick: Sure. We have people of all ages—teenagers, college students, even grandparents!

Nina: Oh, that's great.

Excerpt Two

Rick: OK, good. Because Friendship Force visitors never stay in hotels.

Nina: Oh, that isn't a problem for me. I think living with a family is the best way to learn about a country.

Rick: OK, then.

Excerpt Three

Rick: What country do you want to go to?

Nina: Well, I'm really interested in Thailand.

Rick: Thailand is a beautiful country.

Nina: But what about the language? I only speak English.

Excerpt Four

Nina: Do the visitors have any time to travel?

Rick: Yes, they do. Most visitors spend one or two weeks with their host family first. Then, after that, they travel around the country. But you know, at the Friendship Force, we say, "People, not places" . . .

Nina: Oh . . .

Rick: . . . because we think making new friends is the most important thing.

Nina: I think so, too!

2B. LISTENING TWO: *The Best Summer of my Life!*

Interviewer: Annie, what were the best things about the Experiment in International Living?

Annie: Well, my group was great! And I loved my host family!

Interviewer: Can you tell us about your group?

Annie: Well, we were all high school students from the U.S., but we were very different.

Interviewer: Yes, Experiment groups always have American students from different cities, with different religions and cultures.

Annie: I was excited about that. And, you know, we learned that we weren't really so different!

Interviewer: What do you mean?

Annie: Well, we spent every day together for four weeks. And we learned that people are people. We became such good friends . . . more than friends—we were like a family!

Interviewer: That's wonderful. I'd like to know more about your host family.

Annie: Oh, I loved my host family in Costa Rica. They were so wonderful. They were my family, too! From the first day, I felt like I was their daughter. They called me "Ana."

Interviewer: That's so nice. Did you have any problems speaking with them?

Annie: No, not really. At first, I didn't speak much Spanish, and they spoke only a little English. But I learned a lot of Spanish from them, and in my Spanish class, too. And I also learned that language is not always so important!

Interviewer: What do you mean?

Annie: Well, you know, sometimes a smile can say more than words.

Interviewer: Well, thanks so much, Annie. Do you want to say anything else?

Annie: Yes! If you're in high school, and you want to have a great summer, go on the Experiment! It was the best summer of my life—I'm sure it will be the best summer of your life, too!

Interviewer: Thanks, Annie. That was Annie Quinn, from Philadelphia, Pennsylvania. High school students, you can travel with the Experiment for three, four, or five weeks. Our groups go to 27 different countries. You can study a language, history, culture, dance, sports—almost anything! Please see our website for more information, or for an application.

UNIT 2: Recycled Fashion

2A. LISTENING ONE: *Eco-Fashion*

Interviewer: Today, we're talking with Deborah Lindquist, a famous eco-fashion designer in Los Angeles. Let's start with a basic question: What is eco-fashion?

Lindquist: Eco-fashion is fashion that uses organic materials like wool and cotton. I use organic materials in my eco-fashion, but I also recycle clothes—so for example, I use old saris and kimonos—to make new and unusual clothing.

Interviewer: Saris and Kimonos?

Lindquist: Yes, you know, saris are the beautiful, colorful clothes that women wear in India. And kimonos are the robes that women wear in Japan.

Interviewer: Wow—interesting. I bet the clothes you make are beautiful. So, what other materials do you use?

Lindquist: I use a lot of vintage[1] materials—beautiful materials from the 1940s.

Interviewer: Why do you like using *old* materials? Isn't it strange to use *old* materials to make *new* clothes?

Lindquist: Well, the materials are not just *old*. They're *vintage*. They come from fashions from the past. I think vintage materials are so beautiful. And they're one-of-a-kind. So, the clothes I make are really different. Other people don't have the same clothing.

Interviewer: And if you don't use these materials, they'll just go into the trash, right?

Lindquist: Right. And trash is very bad for the environment. I want people to know that eco-fashion helps the environment. I think more businesses need to help the environment, too.

LISTEN FOR MAIN IDEAS

Interviewer: Today, we're talking with Deborah Lindquist, a famous eco-fashion designer in Los Angeles. Let's start with a basic question: What is eco-fashion?

Lindquist: Eco-fashion is fashion that uses organic materials like wool and cotton. I use organic materials in my eco-fashion, but I also recycle clothes—so for example, I use old saris and kimonos—to make new and unusual clothing.

Interviewer: Saris and Kimonos?

Lindquist: Yes, you know, saris are the beautiful, colorful clothes that women wear in India. And kimonos are the robes that women wear in Japan.

Interviewer: Wow—interesting. I bet the clothes you make are beautiful. So, what other materials do you use?

Lindquist: I use a lot of vintage materials—beautiful materials from the 1940s.

Interviewer: Why do you like using *old* materials? Isn't it strange to use *old* materials to make *new* clothes?

Lindquist: Well, the materials are not just *old*. They're *vintage*. They come from fashions from the past. I think vintage materials are so beautiful. And they're one-of-a-kind. So, the clothes I make are really different. Other people don't have the same clothing.

Interviewer: And if you don't use these materials, they'll just go into the trash, right?

Lindquist: Right. And trash is very bad for the environment. I want people to know that eco-fashion helps the environment. I think more businesses need to help the environment, too.

Interviewer: So, using old clothing is better than throwing it away. But don't most people like to buy new clothes? How many people really like to wear old clothing?

[1]**vintage:** old and showing high quality

Lindquist: A lot of people *love* recycled clothing. They love wearing unusual things, beautiful things.

Interviewer: I guess so, but how many people *really* like eco-fashion? Do you have any idea?

Lindquist: Well, I know that eco-fashion is becoming trendy. More and more stores are selling it. You can see eco-fashion in Europe and Asia now, not only here in the United States.

Interviewer: That's interesting. You say it's all over the world?

Lindquist: Right. There are eco-fashion companies in Denmark, Brazil, the UK . . .

Interviewer: Wow. I didn't know that. So, now that you're in the business, what's your advice for someone who wants to be a fashion designer?

Lindquist: Go to school! I mean it. Go to school! Find a good school and learn as much as you can.

Interviewer: Where did you go to school?

Lindquist: I went to Parsons School of Design in New York City. I loved it!

Interviewer: Wow—New York. OK—can we look at some of your eco-fashion?

Lindquist: Sure. These pictures are from a fashion show in LA . . . Here, the woman is wearing a skirt that I made out of a recycled kimono. You can see some Chinese characters on her skirt.

Interviewer: What about this picture?

Lindquist: The second picture is a jacket. I made it out of some vintage material. See that material? That's very old . . .

Interviewer: It's beautiful. And what about this last picture?

Lindquist: The skirt is a recycled kimono.

Interviewer: That is beautiful!

Lindquist: Yes, I like it, too.

Interviewer: How old is it?

Lindquist: I don't really know.

Interviewer: Where do you get these old kimonos?

Lindquist: *(Laughing)* That's a secret.

Interviewer: Well, thanks for showing me the pictures. Where do you get all your ideas?

Lindquist: I think about eco-fashion all the time. I get new ideas for my designs every day.

Interviewer: And how's your business?

Lindquist: It's great. I do a lot of fashion shows. And my fashion's in a lot of magazines—and also in a lot of stores. People really want to wear beautiful things. And people care about the environment, too.

Interviewer: Well, it was very nice to meet you, Deborah. Thanks for the interview.

Lindquist: You're very welcome.

LISTEN FOR DETAILS

(Listen again to Listen for Main Ideas.)

MAKE INFERENCES

Excerpt One

Interviewer: So, using old clothing is better than throwing it away. But don't most people like to buy new clothes? How many people really like to wear old clothing?

Lindquist: A lot of people *love* recycled clothing. They love wearing unusual things, beautiful things.

Interviewer: I guess so, but how many people *really* like eco-fashion? Do you have any idea?

Excerpt Two

Interviewer: So, now that you're in the business, what's your advice for someone who wants to be a fashion designer?

Lindquist: Go to school! I mean it. Go to school! Find a good school and learn as much as you can.

Excerpt Three

Interviewer: That is beautiful!

Lindquist: Yes, I like it, too.

Interviewer: How old is it?

Lindquist: I don't really know.

Interviewer: Where do you get these old kimonos?

Lindquist: That's a secret.

2B.   LISTENING TWO: *The Quilts of Gee's Bend*

Narrator: Gee's Bend, a small, poor town in Alabama, is making big news in the art world. The big news is quilts—blankets made by hand to keep people warm when they sleep. Now these quilts are in museums; these quilts are works of art. The women who make these quilts don't call them art, but they work just like artists and designers everywhere. They decide how to put all the pieces together, how to make them look beautiful. And they use old materials: old clothes, jeans, pants, dresses because old materials don't cost any money. One woman made a quilt with her husband's old work clothing.

Woman: When he passed away, I made a quilt with his old clothes . . . to remember him that way. I can't believe that quilt's in a museum now. A museum! Those clothes were old. My husband wore them outside, working on the farm, our sweet potato farm.

Narrator: Look at the different kinds of blue in her quilt: dark blue from the pockets, light blue—you can see how these jeans got lighter in the sun. What a beautiful example of recycled material!

Woman: To make a quilt, you put the pieces on the floor. Put the pieces this way and that. See how they work together. Then take another piece, and another. Does that make sense? Sometimes they look good together. Sometimes they don't!

Narrator: At Gee's Bend, the quilts all look different. The women are adding new materials and new colors all the time. They're always making something unusual. And the older women are always teaching the younger women to make quilts.

Woman: My great-grandmother made a quilt with all the colors of Africa. And she said, "Come on now, sit down and eat lunch on this quilt. Let me tell you my story. Listen to the story of my life."

Narrator: Grandmothers teaching granddaughters, mothers teaching daughters—working together for years. In Gee's Bend, a very poor town, the art is rich.

3C. SPEAKING

PRONUNCIATION: Syllables and Stress in Words

Exercise 4

A: What's in the box? Is that a wool coat ?

B: Let's see . . . There's a blanket, some kitchen things, and . . . what's this?

A: A shirt? Maybe a jacket? I can't decide.

B: Let's keep it. The color is nice.

UNIT 3: Rap Music

2A.   LISTENING ONE: *A Famous Rapper: Tupac Shakur*

Eli Jones: King Kool, you were one of the first rappers, back in the 70s.

King Kool: That's right. That's when rap was party music, like that song you just played, "Rapper's Delight."

Eli Jones: So people really danced to rap music?

King Kool: Yeah! The rhythm was great for dancing.

Eli Jones: Uh-huh.

King Kool: The words rhymed, like today's rap songs, but they didn't really mean anything! Y'know, like: "up jump the boogie to the bang bang boogie."

Eli Jones: OK, so when did rap change?

King Kool: Well, in the 80s, young rappers like Tupac Shakur started to write songs about their lives.

LISTEN FOR MAIN IDEAS

Eli Jones: King Kool, you were one of the first rappers, back in the 70s.

King Kool: That's right. That's when rap was party music, like that song you just played, "Rapper's Delight."

Eli Jones: So people really danced to rap music?

King Kool: Yeah! The rhythm was great for dancing.

Eli Jones: Uh-huh.

King Kool: The words rhymed, like today's rap songs, but they didn't really mean anything! Y'know, like: "up jump the boogie to the bang bang boogie."

Eli Jones: OK, so when did rap change?

King Kool: Well, in the 80s, young rappers like Tupac Shakur started to write songs about their lives.

Eli Jones: Uh-huh.

King Kool: And, you know, a lot of rappers came from poor neighborhoods . . . The people there had no jobs, no money . . .

Eli Jones: Mmm-hmm.

King Kool: . . . and young people were angry about that. Tupac was very angry about that. He wanted people to know about those problems. So, he wrote songs about them.

Eli Jones: So the words in his rap songs were important.

King Kool: Absolutely! In my opinion, Tupac Shakur was the greatest songwriter ever. Even better than me!

Eli Jones: Why do you say that?

King Kool: Because his songs were so real!

Eli Jones: Mmm-hmm . . . but some people say his songs were too real.

King Kool: You mean, because he wrote about guns and drugs?

Eli Jones: Yeah, the music that we call "gangsta rap."

King Kool: Well, if you ask me, a lot of people don't understand Tupac. Tupac wrote about the problems he saw every day in his city— and he saw a lot of drugs and guns. But he never said those things were good. He wrote about them because they were in his life.

Eli Jones: Yeah, his songs were about real life.

King Kool: Mmm-hmm. And young African Americans loved Tupac, because his songs told about their lives, too.

Eli Jones: Young people today still love him.

King Kool: Absolutely! Tupac died in 1997, but his music is still popular today.

Eli Jones: You're right. How old was Tupac when he died?

King Kool: He was only twenty-five. But y'know, Tupac always said, "I'm going to die young." He knew it.

Eli Jones: Well, Tupac Shakur is gone, but his music is still alive. King Kool, thanks for speaking with us this evening.

King Kool: My pleasure, Eli.

Eli Jones: And that's it for tonight's show. This is Eli Jones. Good night, and be cool.

LISTEN FOR DETAILS

(Listen again to Listen for Main Ideas.)

MAKE INFERENCES

Excerpt One

Eli Jones: King Kool, you were one of the first rappers, back in the 70s.

King Kool: That's right. That's when rap was party music, like that song you just played, "Rapper's Delight."

Eli Jones: So people really danced to rap music?

King Kool: Yeah! The rhythm was great for dancing.

Excerpt Two

King Kool: And, you know, a lot of rappers came from poor neighborhoods . . . The people there had no jobs, no money . . .

Eli Jones: Mmm-hmm.

King Kool: . . . and young people were angry about that. Tupac was very angry about that. He wanted people to know about those problems. So, he wrote songs about them. . . . In my opinion, Tupac Shakur was the greatest songwriter ever. Even better than me!

Excerpt Three

King Kool: Because his songs were so real!

Eli Jones: Mmm-hmm . . . but some people say his songs were too real.

King Kool: You mean, because he wrote about guns and drugs?

Eli Jones: Yeah, the music that we call "gangsta rap."

Excerpt Four

King Kool: Well, if you ask me, a lot of people don't understand Tupac. Tupac wrote about the problems he saw every day in his city— and he saw a lot of drugs and guns. But he never said those things were good. He wrote about them because they were in his life.

2B. LISTENING TWO: *Rap—Good or Bad?*

The principal of Washington High School invited two people to speak to the Parents' Organization about rap music: Mr. Robbie Simon, a successful music producer, and Professor Brad Crosby, a professor of education.

Principal: Thank you for speaking to our Parents' Organization this evening. I think we all know that rap music is very popular, but, as you know, some parents think that rap is bad. They don't like the words in rap songs, and they don't like what the songs say. Some of them even say that rap isn't real music because the songs have no melody and the rappers don't play any instruments. So they don't want their children to listen to rap music. Mr. Simon, what can you say to these parents?

Mr. Simon: Well, first I want to say that rap music started more than thirty years ago, and it is still very popular today. So, how can people say, "Rap is bad"? In my opinion, a lot of parents don't understand rap music. That's the real problem! Rap is very different from the music that most parents listen to. That's why they think rap is bad. They just can't understand it.

Principal: Professor Crosby, do you agree?

Professor Crosby: No, I do not. I think parents today believe that rap music is bad for a very important reason. Let me explain: Most teenagers think that rappers are cool, so they want to copy them. So, a lot of teens wear hip-hop style clothes and they copy the rappers' language—you know, they use slang and bad words. And then, when they hear rap songs about guns or drugs or sex, they think those things are cool, too. And sometimes they copy what the rappers do, and then they can have a lot of big problems!

Mr. Simon: Oh, come on, Professor! Rap songs tell about real things in the rappers' lives, but they don't say that those things are good! If you ask me, parents have to teach their children what's good and what's bad—not rappers!

Principal: I'd like to say something. We have to remember that there are many different kinds of rap music. All rap is not "gangsta rap"—about guns and killing, like a lot of Tupac Shakur's music. Some rappers, like Kanye West, for example, don't talk about bad things. And Professor Crosby, you probably know that some teachers use rap music in elementary schools . . .

Professor Crosby: Yes, that's true. Some teachers use rap to teach math to young children. The rhythm of the music helps the children to learn and remember more.

Principal: Thank you both for speaking here tonight. I think the discussion about rap will continue for a long time.

3C. SPEAKING

PRONUNCIATION: /ɪ/ vs. /iy/

Exercise 2

1. bit   2. live   3. eat   4. ship   5. seat

UNIT 4: Something Valuable

2A. LISTENING ONE: *The Hope Diamond*

Tour Guide: Here we are—the Hope Diamond. Millions of people come to see this diamond every year. It's the most valuable diamond in the world.

Katelyn: How much is it worth?

Tour Guide: The Hope Diamond is worth 250 million dollars.

Crowd: Wow!

Tour Guide: Yes, it's the most valuable diamond in the world, but that's not all. This diamond has a fascinating history.

LISTEN FOR MAIN IDEAS

Tour Guide: Here we are—the Hope Diamond. Millions of people come to see this diamond every year. It's the most valuable diamond in the world.

Katelyn: How much is it worth?

Tour Guide: The Hope Diamond is worth 250 million dollars.

Crowd: Wow!

Tour Guide: Yes, it's the most valuable diamond in the world, but that's not all. This diamond has a fascinating history.

Bob: Is this the diamond that what's-his-name bought for what's-her-name? You know—the famous movie star's diamond?

Tour Guide: No. King Louis the XIV of France owned this diamond. Imagine . . . it's 1668 and you are Louis the XIV. A man comes to you from India with a huge blue diamond. It is 112 carats! You buy it from him and your jeweler cuts it so it's very beautiful and it sparkles. Now it's 67 carats, and this beautiful jewel is called the "Blue Diamond of the Crown."

Katelyn: Oh, I think I know the rest of the story. Somebody steals it, right?

Tour Guide: Yes. In 1792, somebody steals it and it's gone for a long, long time. Then it appears in London, but it's cut down to 44 carats. It's smaller, but it still has that beautiful clear blue color. Then a wealthy man buys it. His name is Henry Philip Hope, and that's why we call it the Hope Diamond.

Katelyn: Oh, so the name doesn't mean "hope" or "good luck" or anything like that?

Tour Guide: Not at all. Listen to the rest of the story. A wealthy American woman buys it, and then she has some very bad luck.

Katelyn: What happens?

Tour Guide: Well, first her son dies in a car accident, and then her daughter kills herself. And finally—her husband goes crazy!

Bob: That's not because of a diamond! How can a diamond bring bad luck?

Tour Guide: Well, actually, some people think that . . .

LISTEN FOR DETAILS

(Listen again to Listen for Main Ideas.)

MAKE INFERENCES

Excerpt One

Bob: Is this the diamond that what's-his-name bought for what's-her-name? You know—the famous movie star's diamond?

Excerpt Two

Katelyn: Oh, so the name doesn't mean "hope" or "good luck" or anything like that?

Excerpt Three

Bob: That's not because of a diamond! How can a diamond bring bad luck?

2B. LISTENING TWO: *The Four Cs*

Young Adult Male Speaker: Wow, that's a beautiful diamond necklace.

Young Adult Female Speaker: Thanks. It's from Gates Jewelry.

Young Adult Male Speaker: Gates Jewelry? Oh yeah, they advertise on the radio . . .

Narrator: Diamonds . . . diamonds make life more valuable. Wedding day, birthday, any special day is more special with a diamond. At Gates Jewelry, we know our diamonds, and we help *you* find the very best one. At Gates Jewelry, we care about the four Cs. The first C is cut. With the right cut, a diamond really sparkles. The second C is color. Most valuable diamonds have no color at all. The third C is clarity. An excellent diamond is very, very clear. And the fourth C is carat—how much a diamond weighs. At Gates Jewelry you can buy an excellent diamond with all the four Cs at an excellent price. Now *that's* something valuable.

UNIT 5: Together Is Better

2A. LISTENING ONE: *I Remember*

Jane Oliver: Good evening. Welcome to the Alzheimer's Family Meeting. This evening, our speaker is Dr. Alan Dienstag. Dr. Dienstag is a psychologist, and he has started a new support group for people with Alzheimer's disease. It's a writers' group, and I think some of your relatives may want to join it. Please, feel free to ask him questions. Dr. Dienstag, welcome.

LISTEN FOR MAIN IDEAS

Jane Oliver: Good evening. Welcome to the Alzheimer's Family Meeting. This evening, our speaker is Dr. Alan Dienstag. Dr. Dienstag is a psychologist, and he has started a new support group for people with Alzheimer's disease. It's a writers' group, and I think some of your relatives may want to join it. Please, feel free to ask him questions. Dr. Dienstag, welcome.

Dr. Dienstag: Thank you, Ms. Oliver. Hello, everyone. Yes, my new group *is* a writers' group, and it *really is* for people with Alzheimer's. The members of my group get together once a week, and they write stories together.

Relative 1: Excuse me, did you say they write stories?

Dr. Dienstag: Yes, they write stories about their memories. Then they read their stories to the group, and we all talk about them.

Relative 2: Sorry, but . . . my father sometimes doesn't remember my name. How can writing a story help him?

Dr. Dienstag: That's a good question. You see, there are so many things that people with Alzheimer's can't do anymore. You know . . . like work, or drive, or . . . well, a lot of things. But many of them *can* remember their past very well. So, if they can remember something that happened a long time ago and write a story about it, they feel happy.

Relative 2: You mean, because they did something well?

Dr. Dienstag: Yes.

Relative 3: But why . . .

Dr. Dienstag: That's exact . . .

Relative 3: Oh, I'm sorry for interrupting.

Dr. Dienstag: That's alright. Go ahead.

Relative 3: Thanks. Why do they need to meet in a group?

Dr. Dienstag: Well, because, as you know, people with Alzheimer's often forget words. So, they can't always explain their ideas. But when they meet with the group, they can help each other.

Relative 3: Really?

Dr. Dienstag: Yes, it's amazing. Together, they help each other to find the right words to tell their stories. And then they all feel great.

Relative 4: I think that's wonderful. And it's a nice way to make new friends, too, isn't it?

Dr. Dienstag: Yes, and that's very important. So many people with Alzheimer's lose their old friends and they feel lonely. But in the writers' group, the members can *talk* about their feelings. By talking together and writing together, the members become good friends. They really understand each other.

Relative 2: So . . . they write about their memories?

Dr. Dienstag: Yes. Every week, they write about a *different* memory. But they always begin their stories with the same two words: "I remember."

Relative 1: That's interesting. *We* usually think about the things our relatives *don't* remember.

Dr. Dienstag: That's very true. Look, you all know Alzheimer's is a terrible disease. My group members know this, too. But every week, they really enjoy getting together. They like writing, and they always want to read their stories to the group. They like to talk with each other, too, and sometimes they even *laugh* together! Does anyone have any other questions? (pause) OK, then thank you.

Jane Oliver: Thank *you*, Dr. Dienstag.

LISTEN FOR DETAILS

(Listen again to Listen for Main Ideas.)

MAKE INFERENCES

Excerpt One

Dr. Dienstag: Yes, my new group *is* a writers' group, and it *really is* for people with Alzheimer's.

Excerpt Two

Relative 2: Sorry, but my father sometimes doesn't remember my name. How can writing a story help him?

Excerpt Three

Dr. Dienstag: Yes, it's amazing. Together, they help each other to find the right words to tell their stories. And then they all feel great.

Excerpt Four

Relative 4: I think that's wonderful. And it's a nice way to make new friends, too, isn't it?

2B. LISTENING TWO: *Elsa's Story*

Elsa: I remember I was four or five years old, and I looked up and I saw the sky and it looked like an ocean with waves[2], and my mother told me that it was called . . . oh . . . it has a special name . . . The clouds had all these waves, wavy lines . . . ummm . . . Oh dear . . . I can't remember this word . . .

Dr. Dienstag: Was it the nighttime sky or the daytime sky?

Elsa: It was a nice time, I mean, nighttime.

[2]**waves:** areas of raised water that move on the surface of the ocean

Sam: Was it a star?

Elsa: No, it was . . . it had a name . . . Oh, it's on the tip of my tongue! It was a fish . . . It was the name of a fish . . .

Sarah: Was it mackerel sky?

Elsa: Yes! Ah! Mackerel sky! Thank you, Sarah. Mackerel sky . . .

Dr. Dienstag: A mackerel sky, you mean when the clouds look like the waves on the back of a fish—a mackerel?

Elsa: Yes, that's it.

Dr. Dienstag: OK, great, Elsa. Please go on with your story now.

3C. SPEAKING

PRONUNCIATION: /eɪ/ and /ɛ/

Exercise 4

1. **A:** I'm really tired of working.

   B: I am too. Let's take a break and get some coffee.

2. **A:** Can I ask a question?

   B: Absolutely. Go ahead.

3. **A:** What happened? You're really late. Did you get lost?

   B: Yes. I'm sorry. I always forget how to get here.

4. **A:** I don't know anyone here. I feel very uncomfortable.

   B: Don't worry. You'll make friends fast here. Everyone is very friendly.

5. **A:** You told me the test was today. But the teacher said it's tomorrow.

   B: Sorry. I made a mistake. I thought she said today.

6. **A:** Do you want to get together this weekend?

   B: That's a great idea. How about a movie?

UNIT 6: Thinking Young: Creativity in Business

2A.   LISTENING ONE: *K-K Gregory, Young and Creative*

Professor Ray: OK, everyone, let's get started. Today, our guest speaker is K-K Gregory. K-K is a successful business owner, and she's only seventeen years old. Her company makes Wristies. K-K?

K-K Gregory: Hi, . . . umm . . . It's really exciting to be here, in a business school class, because *I'm* still in high school! I'm 17 now, but I started my company when I was 10.

LISTEN FOR MAIN IDEAS

Professor Ray: OK, everyone, let's get started. Today, our guest speaker is K-K Gregory. K-K is a successful business owner, and she's only seventeen years old. Her company makes Wristies. K-K?

K-K Gregory: Hi, . . . umm . . . It's really exciting to be here, in a business school class, because *I'm* still in high school! I'm 17 now, but I started my company when I was 10.

Students' Voices: That's unbelievable! Wow! So young . . .

K-K Gregory: Really! It's true! See? . . . These are Wristies. They're long gloves, but they have no fingers. So they keep your hands and wrists warm and dry, but you can move your fingers easily. You can

wear them outside, for sports or work. But you can also wear them inside, in a cold house or office. There are really a lot of places that you can wear them.

Professor Ray: That's so interesting. K-K, could you tell everyone how you got the idea to make Wristies?

K-K Gregory: Sure. Um . . . As I said, I was 10 years old, and it was winter, and I was playing outside in the snow. I was wearing warm clothes and warm gloves, but my wrists were really cold! And that's when I had the idea. I just thought of it. So I went home and I found some warm material. I put it around my wrists and I made a little hole for my thumb. And that's how I made the first pair of Wristies.

Professor Ray: That's great! Are there any questions? Yes, Nathan?

Student 1: Yeah, um . . . how did you decide to start a business?

K-K Gregory: Well, at first, I didn't think about starting a business at all. I mean, I was only 10! I just made a lot of Wristies in different colors, and I gave them to my friends. They all wore them every day and loved them, and I was happy! But then my friends said, "You know, you can sell these things!" And I thought, "Hmm . . . that could be fun!" So, I asked my mother about it, and she thought it was a great idea. So she helped me to start my company.

Professor Ray: Uh-huh. Did your mother have any business experience?

K-K Gregory: No! My mother didn't know anything about business, and of course I didn't either. So, we talked to a lot of people and we asked a lot of questions, and we learned a lot. There were a few problems in the beginning, but most of the time, we had fun, and . . .

Student 2: Oh, sorry for interrupting, but where do you sell Wristies?

K-K Gregory: Oh, a lot of department stores and clothing stores sell them, and there's also a website. And one time, I went on a TV shopping show. I was really nervous, but it was so exciting—I sold a thousand pairs of Wristies in one hour!

Students: Wow! A thousand pairs.... That's amazing!

K-K Gregory: Yeah, it was! And I had a great time!

Professor Ray: OK, there are just a few minutes left. Is there one more question? Yes? Marla?

Student 3: K-K, do you have any advice for us?

K-K Gregory: Advice? Well, there are a lot of things, but I guess the most important thing is to be creative. You know, don't be afraid to try something new.

Professor Ray: I think that's great advice, K-K. Ms. K-K Gregory— thank you so much for speaking to us today. And good luck!

K-K Gregory: Thank you.

LISTEN FOR DETAILS

(Listen again to Listen for Main Ideas.)

MAKE INFERENCES

Excerpt One

K-K Gregory: Hi, . . . umm . . . It's really exciting to be here, in a business school class, because *I'm* still in high school! I'm 17 now, but I started my company when I was 10.

Students' voices: That's unbelievable! Wow! So young . . .

K-K Gregory: Really! It's true!

Excerpt Two

K-K Gregory: But then my friends said, "You know, you can sell these things!" And I thought, "Hmm . . . that could be fun!" So, I asked my mother about it, and she thought it was a great idea. So she helped me to start my company.

Excerpt Three

K-K Gregory: And one time, I went on a TV shopping show. I was really nervous, but it was so exciting—I sold a thousand pairs of Wristies in one hour!

Students: Wow! A thousand pairs . . . That's amazing!

2B. LISTENING TWO: *A Business Class*

Professor Ray: OK, everybody . . . what can we learn from K-K Gregory? First of all, she found something that *she needed* and *other* people needed, too. Second, she *listened* to other people. Her friends liked Wristies, her mother liked them . . . That's important. You have to talk to people. And then, she decided to start a business. She didn't know anything about business, but she wasn't afraid to try something completely new. Think about this, because this is very important: Children *think* they can do *any*thing—and sometimes they *can*—because they aren't afraid! You know what *our* problem is? We're not children anymore! So we *are* afraid, we're always afraid to make mistakes! In school, at our jobs, making mistakes is bad, right?

Students: Yeah, sure, right . . .

Professor Ray: OK, so then what happens? We don't want to make mistakes, so we stop being creative. We forget how to be creative. But—we can remember how to be creative again. We can—*if* we can remember the feeling of being a child. Now, how do we do that? Well, there are many ways, but one way that I like is to meditate.

Students: What? Meditate? Huh? Really? OK . . .

Professor Ray: So let's try it. OK, now, everybody close your eyes . . . Everybody! Come on . . . Relax . . . relax. Now, think about when you were a child . . . Maybe you were 7, or 10, or 11 . . . Think about a time that you did something new . . . you tried something for the first time . . . and you weren't afraid . . . You did it . . . and you felt so good . . . Try to remember that good feeling . . . Take your time . . . just think . . . When you remember something, open your eyes, and then tell your story to another student. When you're finished, we'll discuss your stories together.

UNIT 7: Planting Trees for Peace

2A. LISTENING ONE: *Wangari Maathai and the Green Belt*

Part One

Narrator: Wangari Maathai understood something important. When her village lost its trees, all the people became hungry. The same thing was happening all over Africa. So Wangari encouraged the women in her village to plant new trees.

Green Belt Spokesperson: *Many* people ask Wangari, "Why is planting trees the best way to help people in Africa?" So she tells them, "It's because planting a tree is so easy. Everyone can do it! Here, watch me. You see? You just make a little hole in the ground . . . like this . . . and you put in a seedling . . . and then you water it. And that's it! Isn't it beautiful? And you know, trees grow quickly here in Africa, so people can have fruit and good soil and wood very soon."

Part One

Narrator: Wangari Maathai understood something important. When her village lost its trees, all the people became hungry. The same thing was happening all over Africa. So Wangari encouraged the women in her village to plant new trees.

Green Belt Spokesperson: Many people ask Wangari, "Why is planting trees the best way to help people in Africa?" So she tells them, "It's because planting a tree is so easy. Everyone can do it! Here, watch me. You see? You just make a little hole in the ground . . . like this . . . and you put in a seedling . . . and then you water it. And that's it! Isn't it beautiful? And you know, trees grow quickly here in Africa, so people can have fruit and good soil and wood very soon."

The women in Wangari's village were very poor. They had no education and no political power. But after they planted new trees, they had hope for a better future. This was very exciting for them! Then, these women went to other villages, and they encouraged the women in other villages to plant trees, too. And then those women encouraged women in other villages. And soon, all over Kenya, women started planting trees. They planted thousands of trees!

Narrator: And that is how Wangari Maathai started the Green Belt Organization, in 1977. The Green Belt encourages women to plant trees in their villages—to make a "green belts of trees." The Green Belt pays women a small amount of money for every seedling they plant. With this money, the women can buy food for their families. Then their children can stay healthy and continue going to school. Since 1977, Green Belt members have planted more than 31 million trees all over the world.

Part Two

Green Belt Spokesperson: But Kenya still had a very serious problem with the environment. Without trees, the people had no food, no water, and no wood. Many, many people were hungry and sick. So we decided to ask our government for help. But our government did not want to help us. At first, we were shocked. But soon we understood what happened. We learned that the president of Kenya gave our land to his friends! They cut down all our trees, and they planted coffee on our land. The president's friends made a lot of money. But they destroyed our land and our life. At that time, we understood that Kenya needed a new government.

Narrator: And so, in the 1990s, Wangari Maathai spoke out all over Kenya. She said that the country needed a new government, a democracy. The president tried to stop Wangari, and he tried to destroy the Green Belt Organization. The police beat Wangari up so badly that she had to go to the hospital. The president put Wangari and many Green Belt members in jail. But Wangari Maathai did not stop speaking out about her ideas.

Green Belt Spokesperson: Everywhere she went, Wangari said this: "We want a clean environment and a good future for our children. Without a democracy, we will continue to lose our land. Then our people will always be poor and hungry. And we will never have peace."

Narrator: This was a new idea for many people. Wangari Maathai said that a good environment and democracy were necessary for peace.

Green Belt Spokesperson: Wangari explained her idea like this: "All over the world, when people don't have enough land or trees or water, they go to war with other countries to get these things. But when we take care of our environment, we plant the seeds of peace.

Part Three

Narrator: In 2002, the Kenyan people chose a new democratic government, and Wangari Maathai became a member of Kenya's Parliament. She received 98% of the vote! And in 2004, Wangari Maathai became the first African woman to receive the Nobel Peace Prize. The Nobel Prize Committee said that Wangari's work with the Green Belt showed the world that the environment, democracy, and peace were all connected.

Green Belt Spokesperson: *(speaking to interviewer)* Well, at first, you know, I think she was shocked! But then she became so excited. I mean, the Nobel Peace Prize! And you know Wangari! As soon as she heard the news, she planted a new tree! By the way, did *you* ever plant a *tree?*

Narrator: Me?

Green Belt Spokesperson: Yes, you *must* plant a tree! Come on, I'll show you . . .

Narrator: OK, OK! This is Robert Jones, on my way to plant a tree in Kenya.

LISTEN FOR DETAILS

(Listen again to Listen for Main Ideas.)

MAKE INFERENCES

Excerpt One

Green Belt Spokesperson: The women in Wangari's village were very poor. They had no education and no political power. But after they planted new trees, they had hope for a better future. This was very exciting for them!

Excerpt Two

Green Belt Spokesperson: But Kenya still had a very serious problem with the environment. Without trees, the people had no food, no water, and no wood. Many, many people were hungry and sick. So, we decided to ask our government for help. But our government did not want to help us. At first, we were shocked.

Excerpt Three

Green Belt Spokesperson: We learned that the president of Kenya gave our land to his friends! They cut down all our trees, and they planted coffee on our land. The president's friends made a lot of money. But they destroyed our land and our life. At that time, we understood that Kenya needed a new government.

Excerpt Four

Green Belt Spokesperson: Wangari explained her idea like this: "All over the world, when people don't have enough land or trees or water, they go to war with other countries to get these things. But when we take care of our environment, we plant the seeds of peace."

2B. LISTENING TWO: *Rigoberta Menchu, a Mayan Leader*

Ruth: Wow, that was a great TV show! Wangari Maathai is an amazing woman. Your class presentation is going to be great.

Sara: Thanks. Who did you choose for your presentation?

Ruth: I picked Rigoberta Menchu Tum. She's from Guatemala.

Sara: Who is she? I've never heard of her.

Ruth: She's a leader for equal rights. She works to get equal rights for poor people in Guatemala, especially the Mayan people.

Sara: The Mayan people?

Ruth: Yeah. The Mayans are the native people in Central America. And a lot of them are very poor. Rigoberta Menchu Tum helps them and she also helps all women to get equal rights.

Sara: Oh . . . I think I read something about her. Did she win the Nobel Peace Prize?

Ruth: Yeah, in 1992. She was the first native person in the world to win the Peace Prize. And she did all of this without any education.

Sara: Really?

Ruth: Yes. She went to elementary school in the countryside, but just for a very short time. Her family was so poor they needed her to work in their fields. She left school when she was only eight years old. After that, she continued to study, but she did it all on her own.

Sara: That's incredible. How did she become an important leader?

Ruth: Well, when Rigoberta was a teenager, her family joined a political organization. The organization wanted to help poor workers. And they wanted to change the government. They wanted a democracy.

Sara: What happened?

Ruth: Well, of course the government wanted to stop that political group. So they put Rigoberta's whole family in jail—her father, her mother, and her brother—and they beat them up. And then later, they killed all of them.

Sara: Oh, how horrible! What happened to Rigoberta?

Ruth: Well, the government wanted to put her in jail, too, so she left Guatemala and she went to Mexico.

Sara: What did she do in Mexico?

Ruth: There were other Guatemalan people there at that time. So, Rigoberta worked with them to bring a democratic government to Guatemala.

Sara: Wow . . . what an incredible woman.

Ruth: Yeah, she became a very important political leader in Guatemala. And even though the government killed her whole family, she never encouraged people to use violence. In her Nobel Peace Prize speech, she said, "We have learned that change cannot come through war."

Sara: Wow, I can understand why she won the Nobel Peace Prize.

Ruth: I know! And listen to this . . . Here it is . . . The Nobel Committee said Rigoberta's life is a "shining example of non-violence." They said she is an example for the whole world to follow.

Sara: That's beautiful. You know, Rigoberta and Wangari Maathai are similar in a lot of ways.

Ruth: Yeah, you're right. We both picked good women to talk about in class!

UNIT 8: Driving You Crazy

2A. LISTENING ONE: *Road Rage*

Instructor: Good evening, class. Welcome to Traffic School. Tonight we have two speakers, John and Marie. They have true stories about road rage—something we hear a lot about today. Road rage means getting very angry at other drivers. Sometimes it's simple. One driver honks the horn at another driver or tries to move ahead of him. But road rage can also be very dangerous. Do you know how many people are killed in the United States because of road rage? More than 200 people every year. And 12,000 more are injured. This is one of the most serious driving problems.

LISTEN FOR MAIN IDEAS

Instructor: Good evening, class. Welcome to Traffic School. Tonight we have two speakers, John and Marie. They have true stories about road rage—something we hear a lot about today. Road rage means getting angry at other drivers. Sometimes it's simple. One driver honks the horn at another driver or tries to move ahead of him. But road rage can also be very dangerous. Do you know how many people are killed in the United States because of road rage? More than 200 people every year. And 12,000 more are injured. This is one of the most serious driving problems.

John: Last year I was driving home from work, and I almost got killed. It was late. Do you know how it feels when you're really tired? Well, I changed lanes on the highway, and I forgot to use my signal. Suddenly, I saw a bright light behind me. This guy in a big truck was right behind me. He was following me. I was scared, so I started going a little faster. He went faster, too. He was coming after me! I got off the highway and drove into the parking lot of a big supermarket. He followed me into the parking lot. I thought he was going to hit my car with his truck. But he didn't. He just drove right past me, yelling at me. Then he left. I was really lucky.

Instructor: John *was* lucky. Sometimes people actually try to hit other people with their cars. This driver probably didn't hit John because there were other people in the parking lot. They could see him, so he wasn't anonymous anymore. That's one reason for road rage—people feel anonymous in their cars. Nobody knows who they are. They can do things that they usually don't do. Like Marie, for example. She looks like a very nice person. But listen to what she did last year—before she learned how to control her road rage.

Marie: Well, I was driving to work when I saw this man in a red sports car. He was crossing the intersection. I let him go ahead of me and get on the highway first. Usually people wave at you to say "thanks," but he didn't. He just drove away. I don't really know why, but I got very, very angry at him. Why didn't he thank me? I got behind him on the highway, and I tailgated him. We were going about 60 miles an hour and I stayed right behind him. I knew it was dangerous, but I didn't care. Finally I passed him, driving fast and honking at him. You know what? I still can't believe him! He's the rudest guy on the road! Driving around in his sports car, thinking he's better than other people . . . Ugh! If I ever see him again, I'll—

Instructor: Thank you, Marie. In conclusion tonight, I want to tell you that more and more people are driving dangerously. They are stressed out by their jobs, and they sometimes have to drive a long way to work. And the roads are more crowded today—70 percent of the highways in American cities are very, very crowded. More driving, more traffic, more stress—this is why we have road rage. What can you do? You can't control the other driver. You can only control yourself. So, be a safe driver. Be polite. Don't tailgate; don't forget to signal. And if someone makes you angry, forget about it. Turn on the radio; listen to music. Remember: You have only one life. Don't lose it to road rage.

LISTEN FOR DETAILS

(Listen again to Listen for Main Ideas.)

MAKE INFERENCES

Excerpt One

John: Last year I was driving home from work, and I almost got killed. It was late. Do you know how it feels when you're really tired? Well, I changed lanes on the highway, and I forgot to use my signal. Suddenly, I saw a bright light behind me. This guy in a big truck was right behind me. He was following me. I was scared, so I started going a little faster. He went faster, too. He was coming after me! I got off the highway and drove into the parking lot of a big supermarket. He followed me into the parking lot. I thought he was going to hit my car with his truck.

Excerpt Two

Marie: Well, I was driving to work when I saw this man in a red sports car. He was crossing the intersection. I let him go ahead of me and get on the highway first. Usually people wave at you to say "thanks," but he didn't. He just drove away. I don't really know why, but I got very, very angry at him . . . Finally I passed him, driving fast and honking at him . . . Ugh! If I ever see him again . . .

Excerpt Three

Instructor: In conclusion tonight, I want to tell you that more and more people are driving dangerously. They are stressed out by their jobs, and they sometimes have to drive a long way to work. And the roads are more crowded today—70 percent of the highways in American cities are very, very crowded. More driving, more traffic, more stress—this is why we have road rage. What can you do? You can't control the other driver. You can only control yourself.

2B.   LISTENING TWO: *Driving Phobia*

Psychologist: Come on, Allen. You can do it. We talked about this. You know what to do.

Allen: I know. I know what to do, but I just can't do it.

Psychologist: Now what is it, Allen? What exactly are you scared of?

Allen: I don't know. I just hate crossing the bridge. I don't want to do it.

Psychologist: Come on, Allen. You can do it. Think of all the other things you do: your job, your sports, your music. You're very good at everything you do. You can do this, too.

Allen: Too many trucks.

Psychologist: What did you say?

Allen: I'm scared of the trucks! The trucks are going to hit me!

Psychologist: They're not going to hit you, Allen. Don't look at the trucks. The best thing to do is just look at the road.

Allen: I can't. There's too much water! What if we fall?

Psychologist: Don't think of the water, Allen. Just look at the road. Look straight ahead.

Allen: Oh no, we're on the bridge!

Psychologist: Keep looking at the road, Allen. Look straight ahead. You're doing fine. Keep going. You're doing fine. There! You did it! You crossed the bridge!

Allen: *We* crossed the bridge. I can't do it alone.

Psychologist: You will, Allen. You will. Now keep going . . .

UNIT 9: Only Child—Lonely Child?

2A.   LISTENING ONE: *Changing Families*

Maria Sanchez: Hello! Welcome to "Changing Families." I'm Maria Sanchez, and today we're going to talk about only children. In the past, people thought that an only child was a lonely child. But now, more and more families all over the world are deciding to have just one child, especially in big cities. Today, we are going to meet two families with only children. First, we're going to talk with Marion and Mark Carter, from Chicago, Illinois. Hello!

LISTEN FOR MAIN IDEAS

Maria Sanchez: Hello! Welcome to "Changing Families." I'm Maria Sanchez, and today we're going to talk about only children. In the past, people thought that an only child was a lonely child. But now, more and more families all over the world are deciding to have just one child, especially in big cities. Today, we are going to meet two families with only children. First, we're going to talk with Marion and Mark Carter, from Chicago, Illinois. Hello!

Mark and Marion: Hi. Hi, Maria.

Maria: Welcome! Please tell us—Why did you decide to have just one child?

Mark: Well, um . . . we were both thirty-six when we got married . . .

Maria: Uh-huh.

Marion: . . . and then, when I had Tonia, our daughter, we were thirty-eight. Tonia is so wonderful, and we love her more than anything. But . . . well, it's not easy to raise a young child at our age.

Mark: That's for sure. We're always tired!

Maria: I think many young parents feel the same way, too!

Mark: Mmm . . . Maybe . . . Anyway, at some point, we just knew that we couldn't take care of Tonia *and* a new baby.

Marion: Yeah. We decided that we were happy with our little family, and that one child was enough for us.

Maria: OK, that's great. And how does Tonia feel about your family? Is she ever lonely?

Marion: Um . . . I don't think so, because we spend a *lot* of time with her, and she has lots of friends.

Mark: That's for sure! She's very popular!

Maria: Really! You know, that's interesting because I just read that only children are often more popular—and more intelligent—than children with siblings.

Mark: Yes, that IS interesting!

Maria: Isn't it? It's really something to think about. OK, thank you, Marion and Mark. And now, let's say hello to Tom and Jenna Mori from New York City.

Tom and Jenna: Hi, Maria! Hi.

Maria: Now, Tom and Jenna, you also decided to have only one child.

Tom: Yes, that's right . . .

Maria: Can you tell us why?

Tom: Well, it was a hard decision for us . . .

Jenna: Yeah, very hard . . .

Tom: . . . because Jenna and I really love kids. We're both teachers. But, as I'm sure you know, teachers don't make a lot of money!

Maria: That's true. Most teachers aren't rich!

Jenna: Y'know, before we had a child, money wasn't really so important to us.

Maria: That's interesting . . .

Jenna: But now . . . well, when you have a child, it's different. We want our son Jay to have a good life—you know—a good school, piano lessons, travel . . . And those things are very expensive!

Maria: You're right about that!

Tom: Yeah, and we know we can't afford all of those things for *two* children. So we decided to have only one child, so we can give him the best.

Maria: I understand. But do you think Jay wants a sibling? Does he ever feel lonely?

Tom: Jay?! Never!

Jenna: Oh, no. He's always so busy with his friends.

Tom: Yeah, and he does sports, and he plays music.

Maria: Well, that's wonderful! Tom and Jenna Mori—thanks for talking with us.

Tom and Jenna: Our pleasure. Thank *you!*

Maria: OK, next, I'm going to talk to the kids! Don't go away!

LISTEN FOR DETAILS

(Listen again to Listen for Main Ideas.)

MAKE INFERENCES

Excerpt One

Mark: Anyway, at some point, we just knew that we couldn't take care of Tonia *and* a new baby.

Excerpt Two

Maria: You know, that's interesting because I just read that only children are often more popular—and more intelligent—than children with siblings.

Mark: Yes, that IS interesting!

Excerpt Three

Jenna: Y'know, before we had a child, money wasn't really so important to us.

Maria: That's interesting . . .

Jenna: But now . . . well, when you have a child, it's different. We want our son Jay to have a good life—you know—a good school, piano lessons, travel . . . And those things are very expensive!

2B.   LISTENING TWO: *How Do Only Kids Feel?*

Maria Sanchez: Welcome back. What do kids think about being an only child? Let's find out right now! I'm going to speak to Marion and Mark's daughter, Tonia, and to Tom and Jenna's son, Jay. Hi, Tonia.

Tonia: Hi.

Maria: How old are you, sweetheart?

Tonia: Eight.

Maria: Eight. And Jay, you are . . . ?

Jay: I'm thirteen.

Maria: OK. Now Tonia, you're the only child in your family, right?

Tonia: Uh-huh.

Maria: And is that OK with you?

Tonia: No! I hate it . . .

Maria: Really . . . Why?

Tonia: Because I want a sister.

Maria: Oh . . .

Tonia: All my friends have brothers and sisters. I'm the only kid in my class who doesn't have one!

Maria: Oh, I see . . . um . . . Did you ever talk to your mom and dad about it?

Tonia: Yeah, I talked to my mom.

Maria: And what did she say?

Tonia: She said, "I am 46 years old. I am not going to have another child."

Maria: And how did you feel then?

Tonia: I was sad.

Maria: But can you understand your mom and dad?

Tonia: Yeah.

Maria: Well, that's good.

Tonia: But I still want a sister!

Maria: Well, here's a little girl who knows what she wants! Thanks, Tonia. And Jay, how about you? Do you feel the same way?

Jay: No, not at all. I like my family like this.

Maria: Mmhm . . . But do you ever feel lonely?

Jay: No, I don't feel lonely. I feel special! I do a lot of things together with my parents. We always have fun together.

Maria: What kinds of things do you do with your parents?

Jay: Well, the best thing is that we travel a lot. Like, last year, we went to Europe. And this winter, we're going to go skiing in Colorado.

Maria: Wow, that's great!

Jay: Yeah, and I think it's easier for us to do all of these things because it's just the three of us.

Maria: You mean, because your parents can afford it, right?

Jay: Yes, uh-huh . . .

Maria: But do you ever feel different from your friends?

Jay: No. Actually, a lot of my friends are only children, too.

Maria: How interesting . . . Thanks Jay, and thanks to you, too, Tonia.

Tonia and Jay: You're welcome.

Maria: Well, there you have it—two children, and two very different opinions about being an only child. Thanks for watching!

UNIT 10: The Beautiful Game

2A. LISTENING ONE: *The Sports File*

Gooool!

It's a goal!

Goooool!

Jane: That is the sound of soccer. Soccer is the world's favorite sport. Soccer is not very popular in the U.S. But the World Cup is starting, and once again, Americans see that people from all over the world love this game. Pele, the famous Brazilian soccer player, called it "The Beautiful Game." To help us understand why the rest of the world loves soccer, we went to Paolinho's Pizza Restaurant in Minneapolis, Minnesota, for the first match of World Cup soccer.

LISTEN FOR MAIN IDEAS

Gooool!

It's a goal!

Goooool!

Jane: That is the sound of soccer. Soccer is the world's favorite sport. Soccer is not very popular in the U.S. But the World Cup is starting, and once again, Americans see that people from all over the world love

this game. Pele, the famous Brazilian soccer player, called it "The Beautiful Game." To help us understand why the rest of the world loves soccer, we went to Paolinho's Pizza Restaurant in Minneapolis, Minnesota, for the first match of World Cup soccer.

Jane: Excuse me. What is your name, and where are you from?

Gilberto: I am Gilberto, and I am from Brazil.

Jane: Why do you like soccer, Gilberto?

Gilberto: Why? Ha ha! That is not even a question in Brazil. Soccer is our life. It is an art. It's like music—no one asks you, "Why do you like music?!" Music is just part of everyday life, right? In soccer, the ball flies through the air, and when the player jumps into the air, it's like he's flying—like a bird or a dancer. And when he heads³ the ball into the goal, it is simple and beautiful. It is perfect, just like art.

Jane: Thank you Gilberto. And what about you, sir, where are you from?

Jose: I am Jose from Mexico City.

Jane: And why do you watch soccer, Jose?

Jose: Why? Because soccer is like a universal language. I come here to watch soccer, and for example, I don't know this guy's name here— What's your name?

Anders: Anders.

Jose: Yes, Anders—he's from Germany. And I don't really know him, but we are both for Italy today. You see, I'm Mexican, he's German, but we are all soccer fans. It is the same with the teams. For example, a lot of the French players come from Africa and other places, but it's one team on the soccer field. Nationality doesn't matter. There are really only two countries: the country that loves soccer and the country that doesn't understand.

Anders: That's the United States—the country that doesn't understand!

Jane: Well, we're trying! That's why I'm talking to you today! Anders, Jose said you're from Germany?

Anders: Yes, I'm from Berlin.

Jane: And what do you like about soccer?

Anders: Soccer is a game for *everybody*. You don't need money or a lot of equipment—just people, a ball, and a goal. Also, everyone understands it—not like American football. You have to read books to understand all of the rules in American football, even if you are only watching it. Soccer is clear and it's so much fun to watch.

Jane: So *there* are a few reasons to love soccer. The World Cup continues for three more weeks. If you still don't understand why soccer is so popular, maybe you should go and watch a game or two at a restaurant like Paolinho's. You might even become a fan! With The Sports File, this is Jane Tuttle.

LISTEN FOR DETAILS

(Listen again to Listen for Main Ideas.)

MAKE INFERENCES

Excerpt One

Jane: To help us understand why the rest of the world loves soccer, we went to Paolinho's Pizza Restaurant in Minneapolis, Minnesota, for the first match of World Cup soccer.

³**head:** to hit the ball with your head

Excerpt Two

Jose: There are really only two countries: the country that loves soccer and the country that doesn't understand.

Excerpt Three

Jane: If you still don't understand why soccer is so popular, maybe you should go and watch a game or two at a restaurant like Paolinho's. You might even become a fan!

2B.   LISTENING TWO: *America Talks*

Commentator: Welcome to "America Talks." We are taking calls from sports fans all over the country this morning. We want to hear your opinions about soccer: Why isn't soccer popular in the United States? The World Cup is happening right now. About 700 million people all over the world are going to watch the final match on television. But many Americans, even sports fans, do not even know that it is happening. How can Americans NOT be interested in a game that the rest of the world loves—a game that is universal? Our first caller is Bob from Kearny, New Jersey. Welcome to the show, Bob.

Bob: Thanks for taking my call.

Commentator: Bob, why isn't soccer popular in this country?

Bob: Well, I think it's mostly because of the score. You can have a great soccer match, but the final score can be zero to one. I think Americans like to see high scores—they like the numbers to say more about the teams.

Commentator: Interesting point. People also say that ties are a problem for sports fans in the U.S. We really like to have a winner.

Bob: Yeah, I agree.

Commentator: Thanks for the call, Bob. Next, we have Steve from Rochester, New York, on the line. Hello, Steve.

Steve: Hi. You know, I think the main reason soccer isn't popular here is that most of us just didn't grow up with it. Maybe we played a little when we were kids, but we never watched it on TV or listened to it on the radio with our families.

Commentator: So you think it is just that soccer is not a tradition in this country?

Steve: Yeah. Our traditions in the U.S. are baseball, football, and basketball. And if you watch all three of these sports, you're pretty busy. We don't really need another sport.

Commentator: Thanks for your comments, Steve. We have one more call, from Drew in Seattle, Washington. Go ahead, Drew.

Drew: Well, you know Americans love stars. But we haven't had any really big soccer stars here yet. Pele came to play in the U.S. in 1975, and he was a star on the field, but not off the field. And that was a long time ago. Some people say David Beckham is going to get Americans interested in soccer. He IS a star—both on the field and off. He has the Hollywood life. He really might help soccer in the U.S.

Commentator: Yes, I've heard that, too. It could happen. I guess we'll see. Thanks for your call, Drew.

THE PHONETIC ALPHABET

Consonant Symbols

/b/	**b**e		/t/	**t**o
/d/	**d**o		/v/	**v**an
/f/	**f**ather		/w/	**w**ill
/g/	**g**et		/y/	**y**es
/h/	**h**e		/z/	**z**oo, bu**s**y
/k/	**k**eep, **c**an		/θ/	**th**anks
/l/	**l**et		/ð/	**th**en
/m/	**m**ay		/ʃ/	**sh**e
/n/	**n**o		/ʒ/	vi**s**ion, A**s**ia
/p/	**p**en		/tʃ/	**ch**ild
/r/	**r**ain		/dʒ/	**j**oin
/s/	**s**o, **c**ircle		/ŋ/	lo**ng**

Vowel Symbols

/ɑ/	f**a**r, h**o**t		/iy/	**we**, m**ea**n, f**ee**t
/ɛ/	m**e**t, s**ai**d		/ey/	d**ay**, l**a**te, r**ai**n
/ɔ/	t**a**ll, b**ou**ght		/ow/	g**o**, l**ow**, c**oa**t
/ə/	s**o**n, **u**nder		/uw/	t**oo**, bl**ue**
/æ/	c**a**t		/ay/	t**i**me, b**uy**
/ɪ/	sh**i**p		/aw/	h**ou**se, n**ow**
/ʊ/	g**oo**d, c**ou**ld, p**u**t		/oy/	b**oy**, c**oi**n

CREDITS